DECEMBER 50 COLORING PAGES
FOR ADULTS RELAXATION

SHIH CHIEN HUA

I0481757

PUBLISHED BY:
SHIH CHIEN HUA
Copyright © 2018

SEABIRD SHOP >50FOR

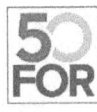

FB FAN PAGE

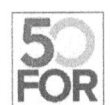

Disclaimer
The information contained in this book is for general information purposes only. The information is provided by the authors and while we endeavor to keep the information up to date and correct, we make no representations or warranties of any kind, express or implied, about the completeness, accuracy, reliability, suitability or availability with respect to the book or the information, products, services, or related graphics contained in the book for any purpose. Any reliance you place on such information is therefore strictly at your own risk.

DECEMBER 1ST

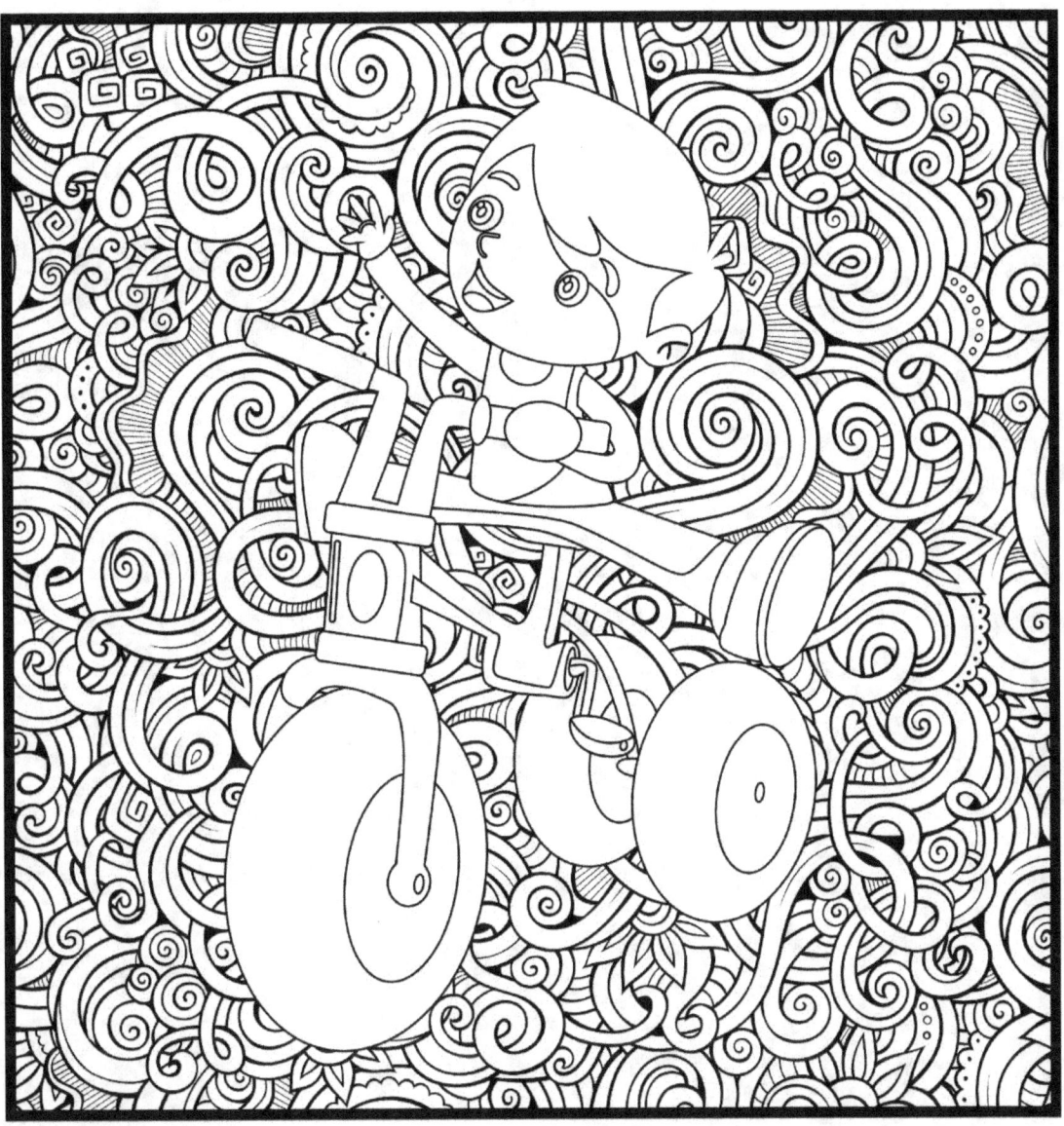

note:

_____

_____

_____

DECEMBER 2ND

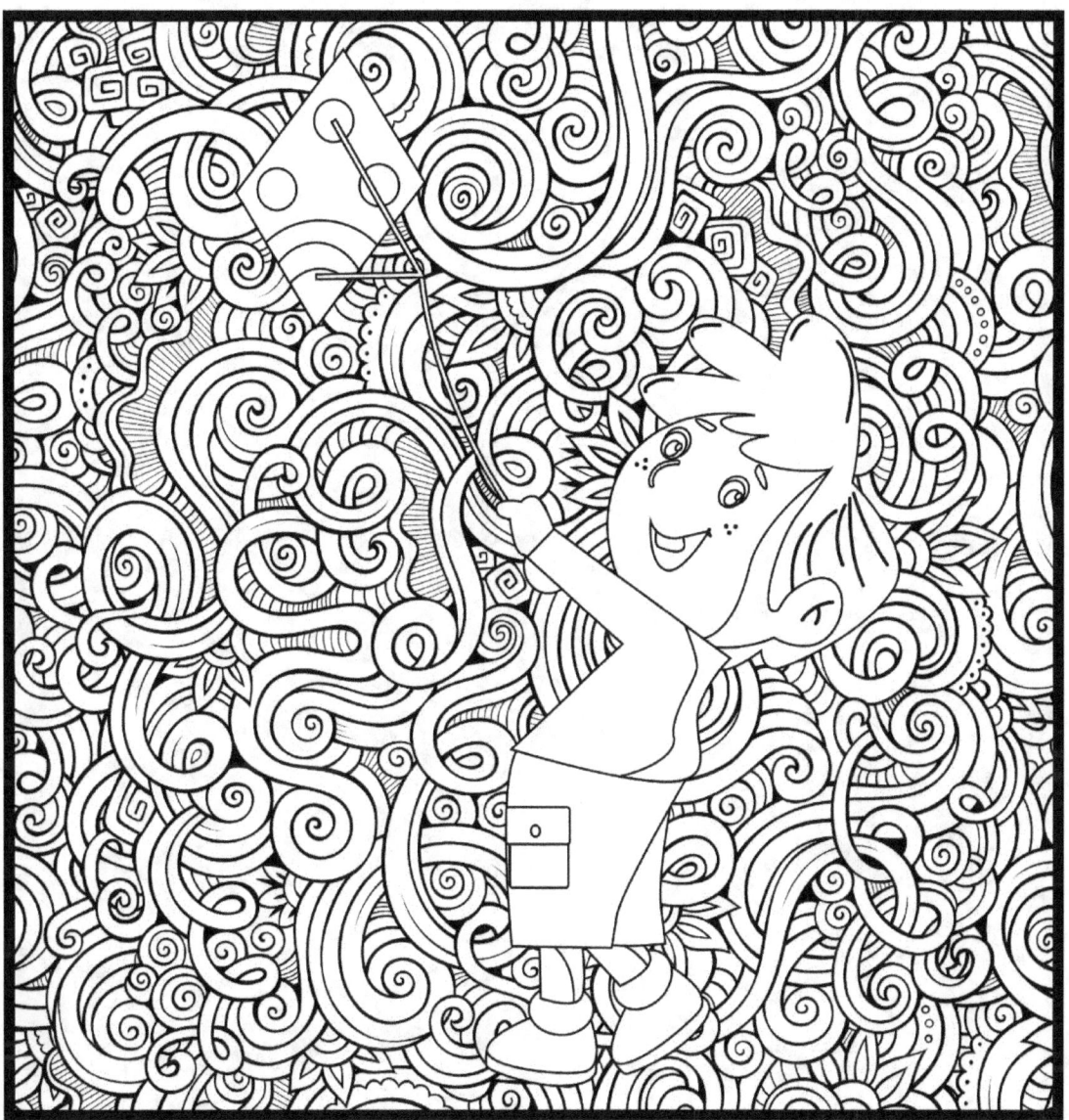

note:

_____

_____

_____

DECEMBER 3RD

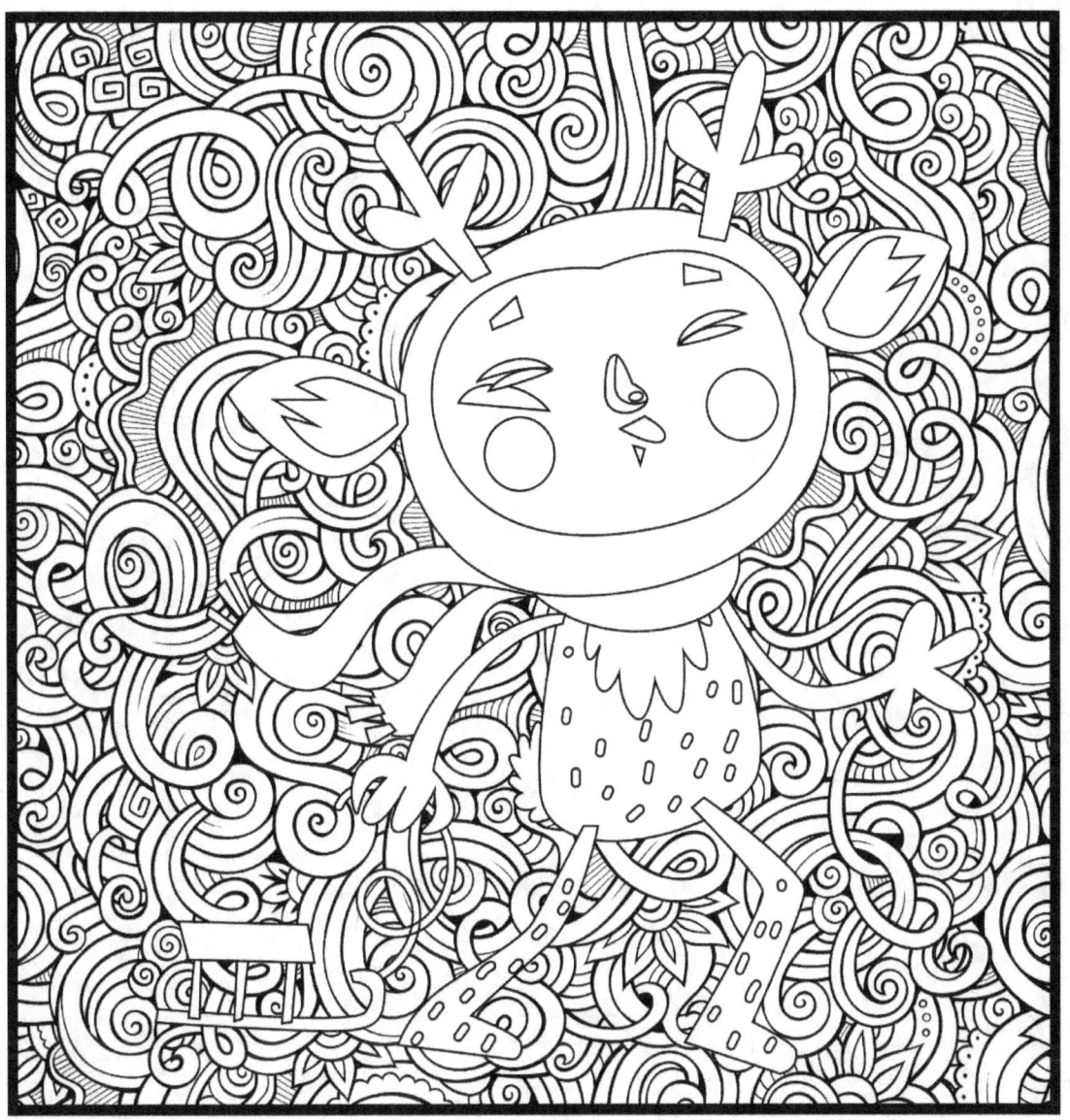

note:

_____

_____

_____

DECEMBER 4TH

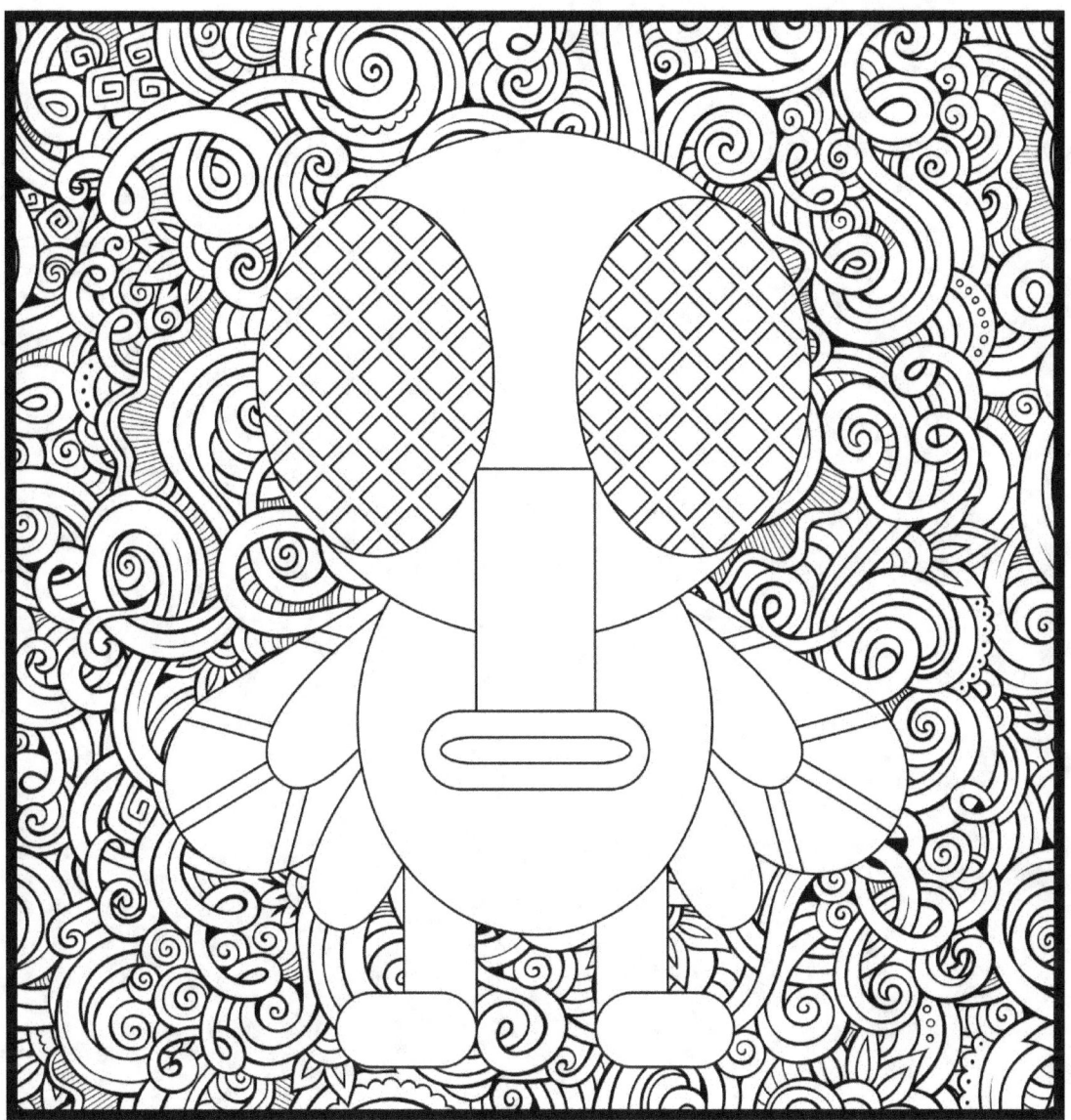

note:

_____

_____

_____

DECEMBER 5TH

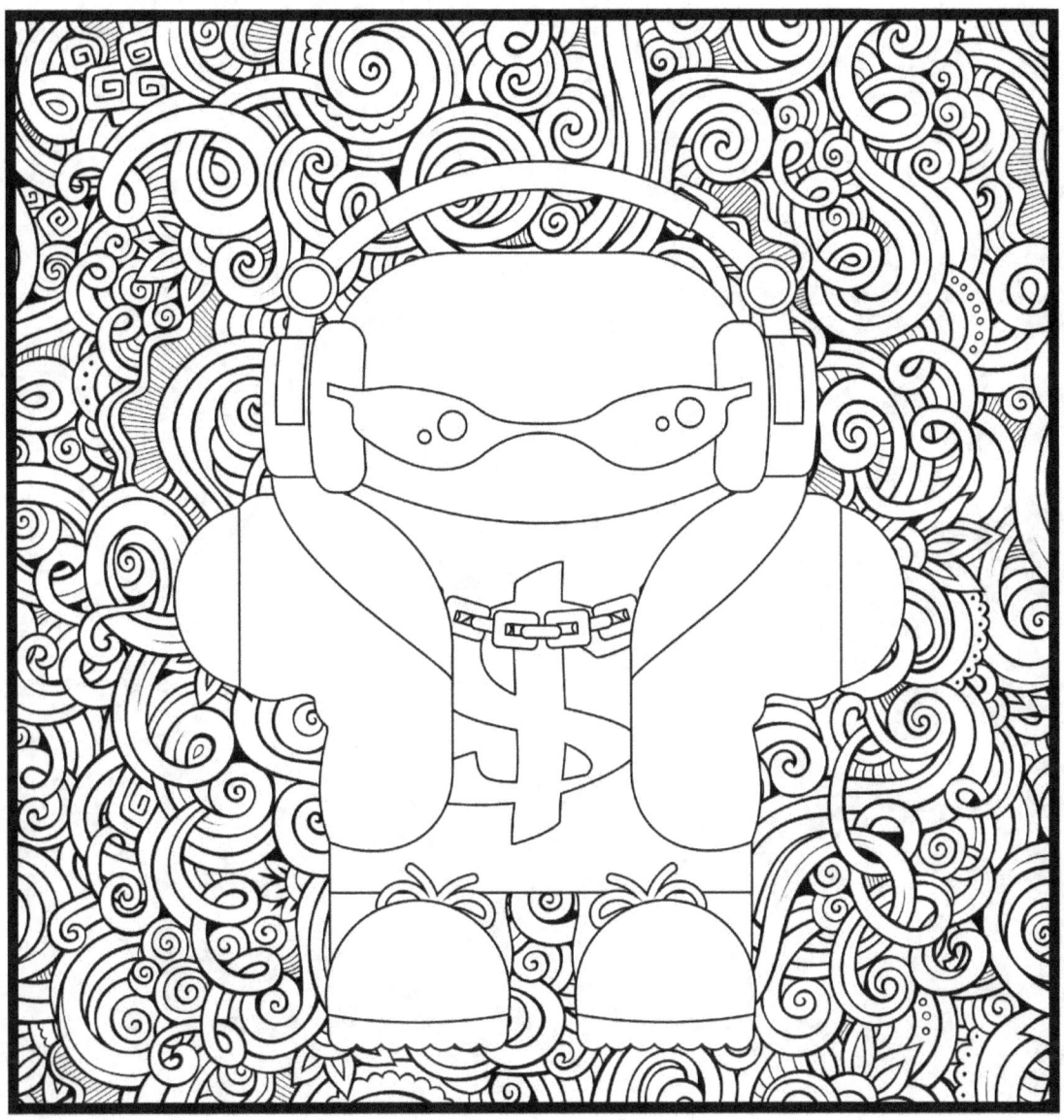

note:

_____

_____

_____

DECEMBER 6TH

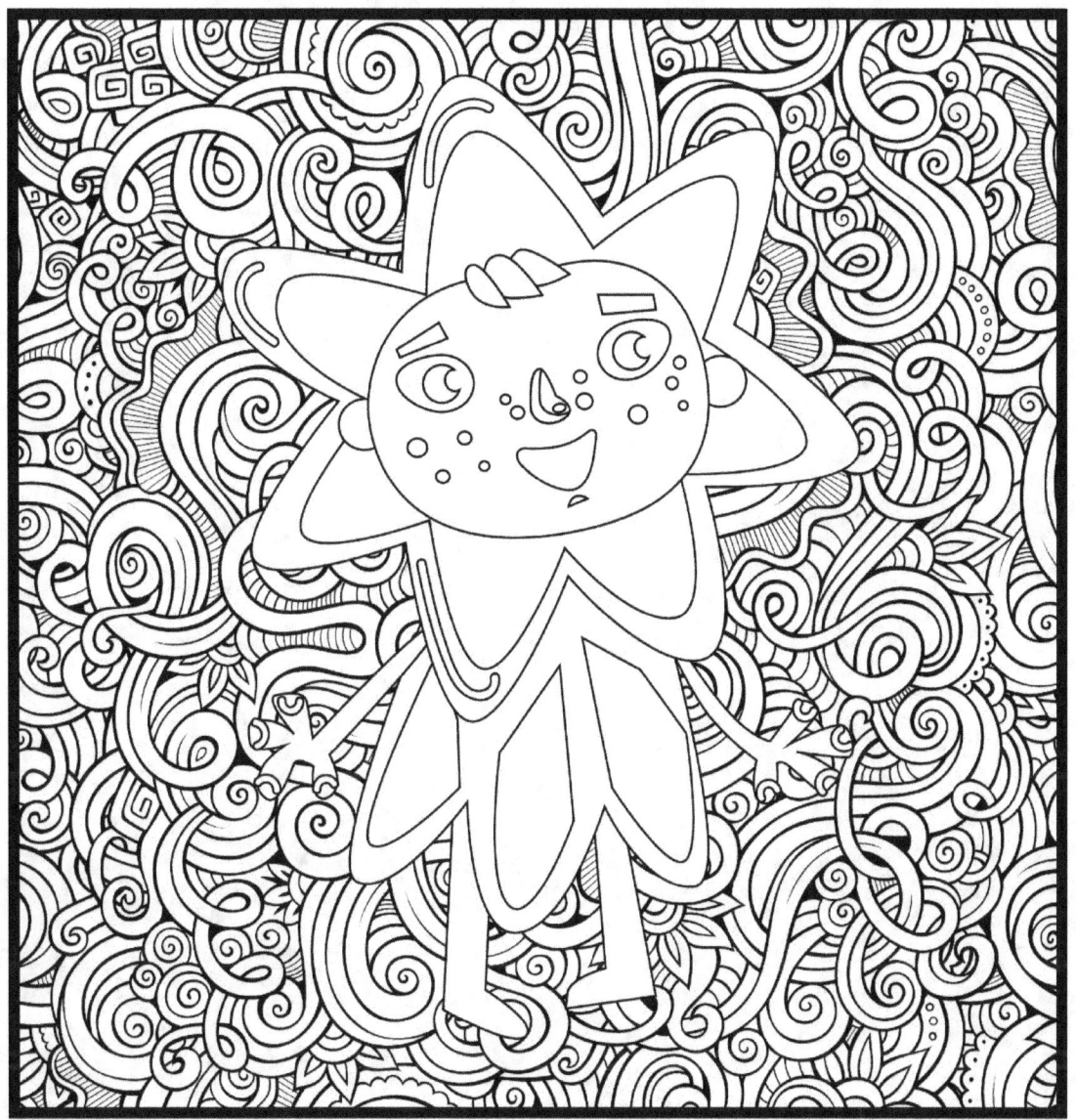

note:

_____

_____

_____

DECEMBER 7TH

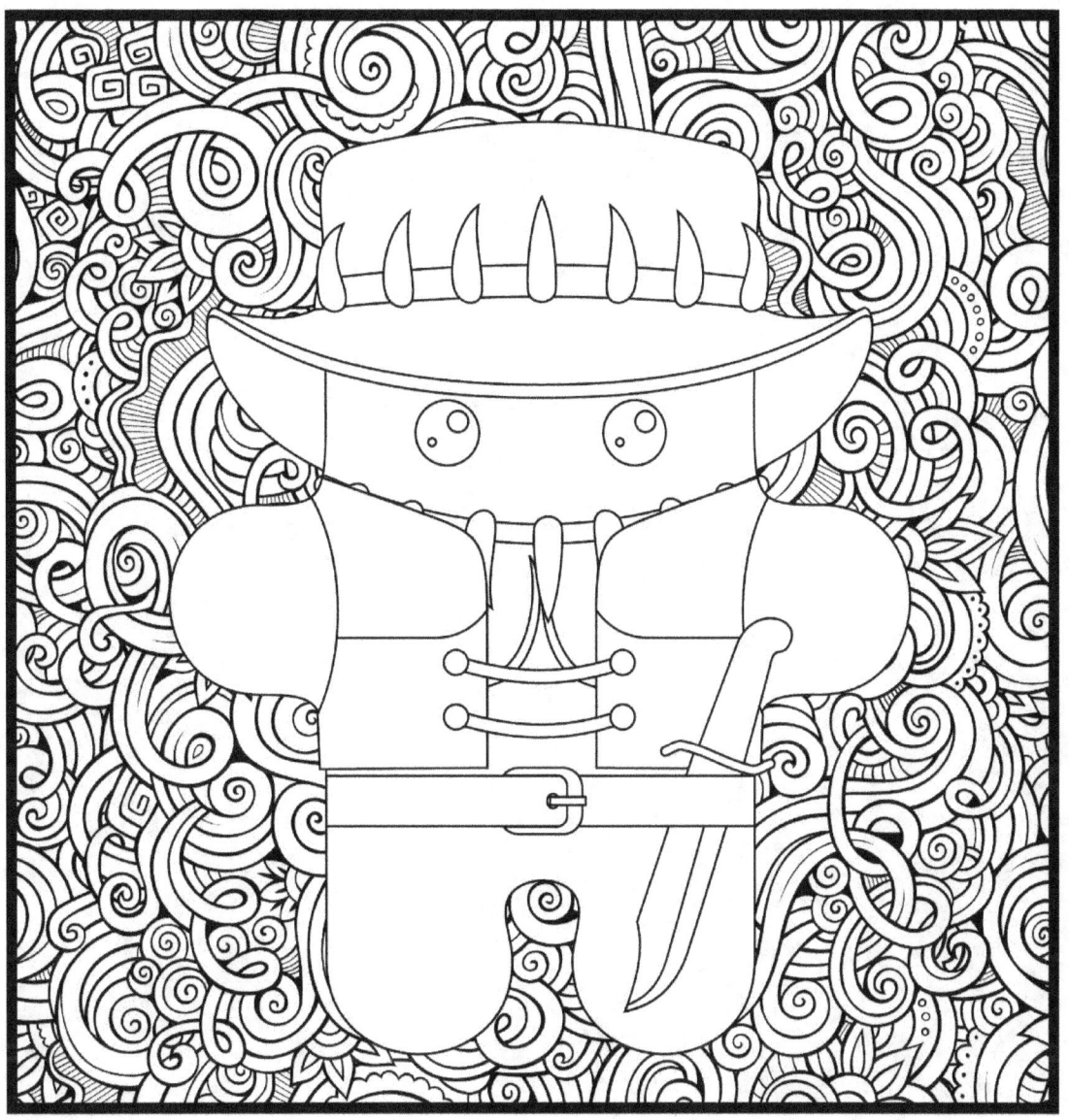

note:

_____

_____

_____

DECEMBER 8TH

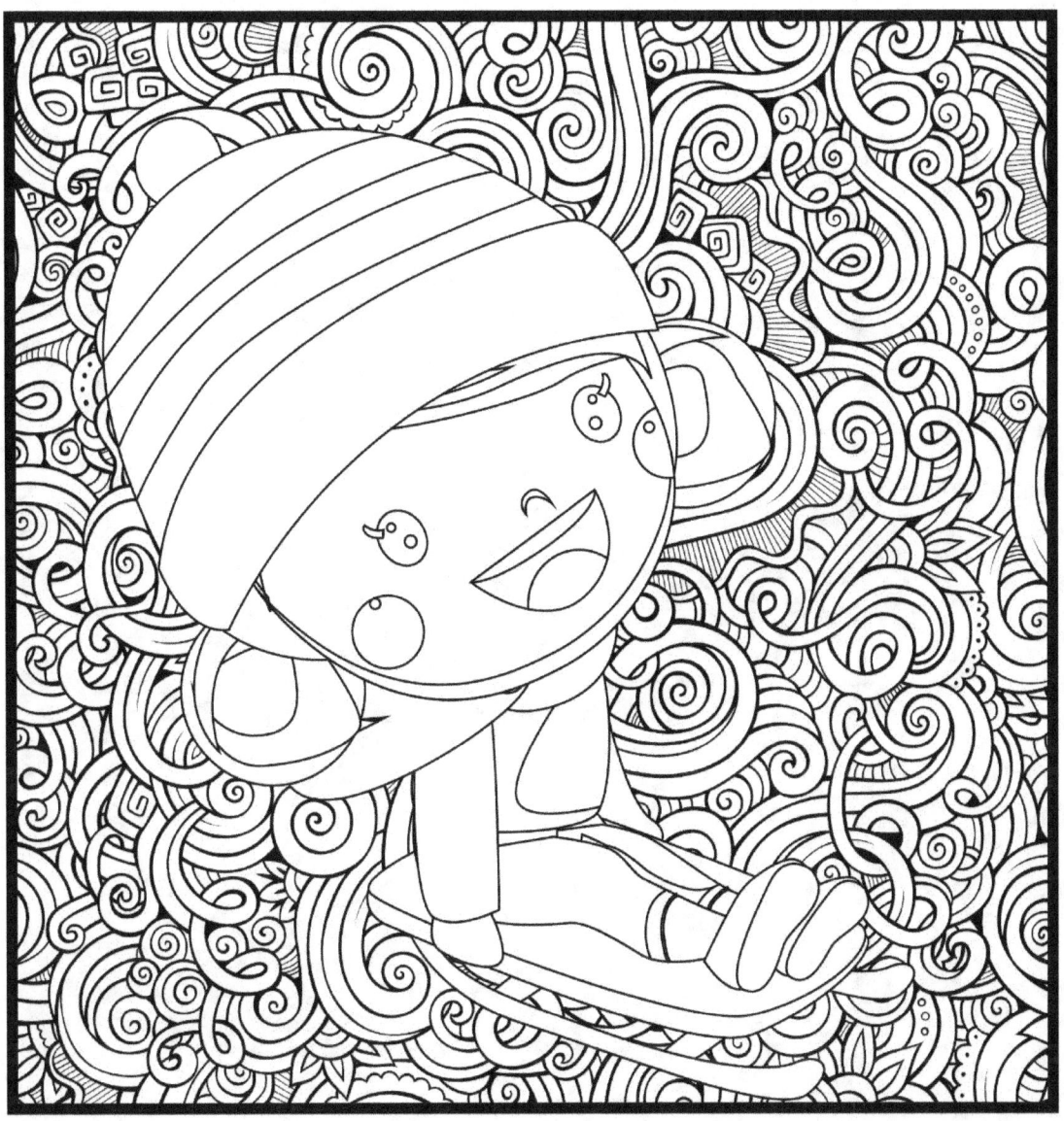

note:

_____

_____

_____

DECEMBER 9TH

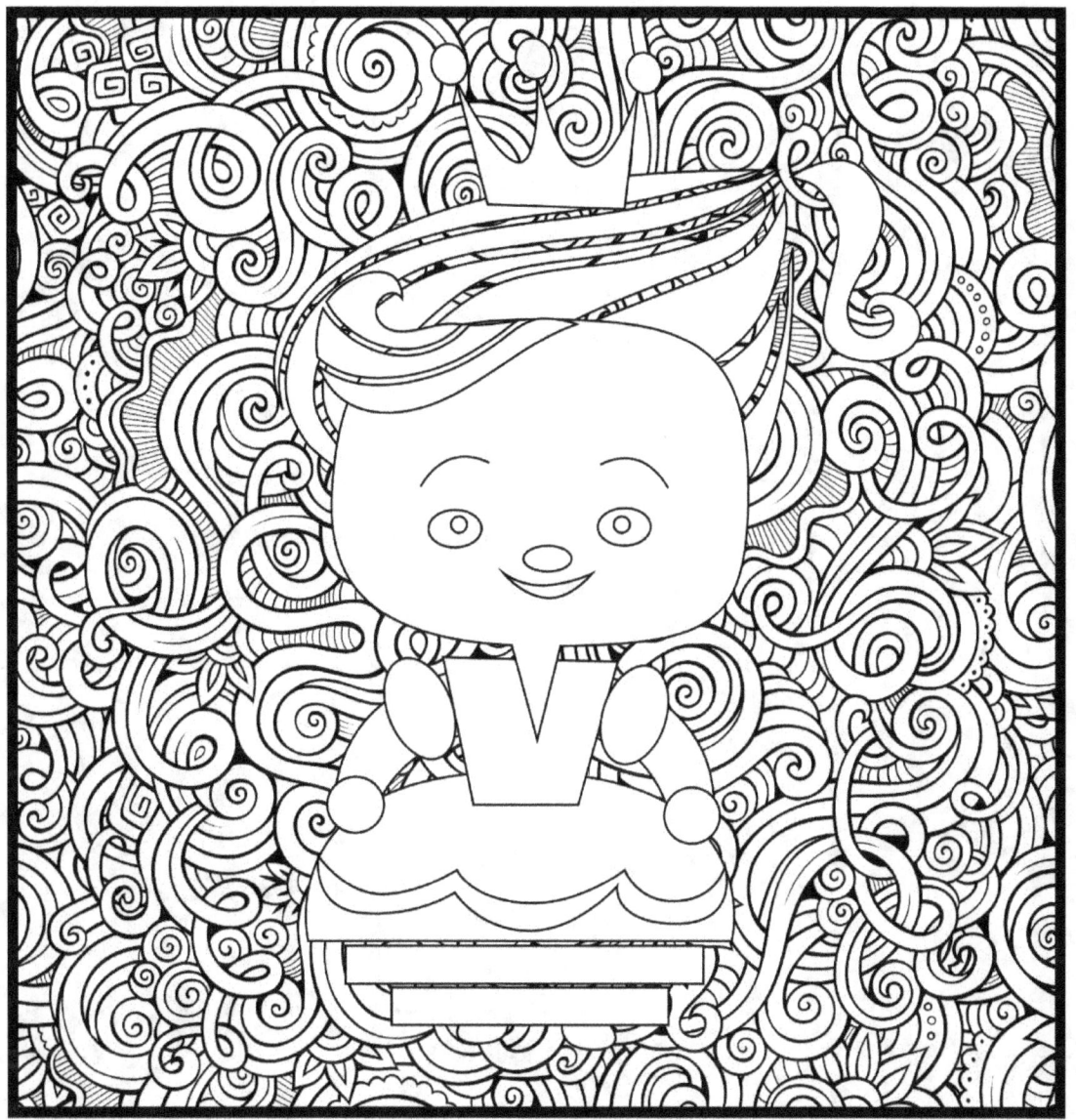

note:

_____

_____

_____

DECEMBER 10TH

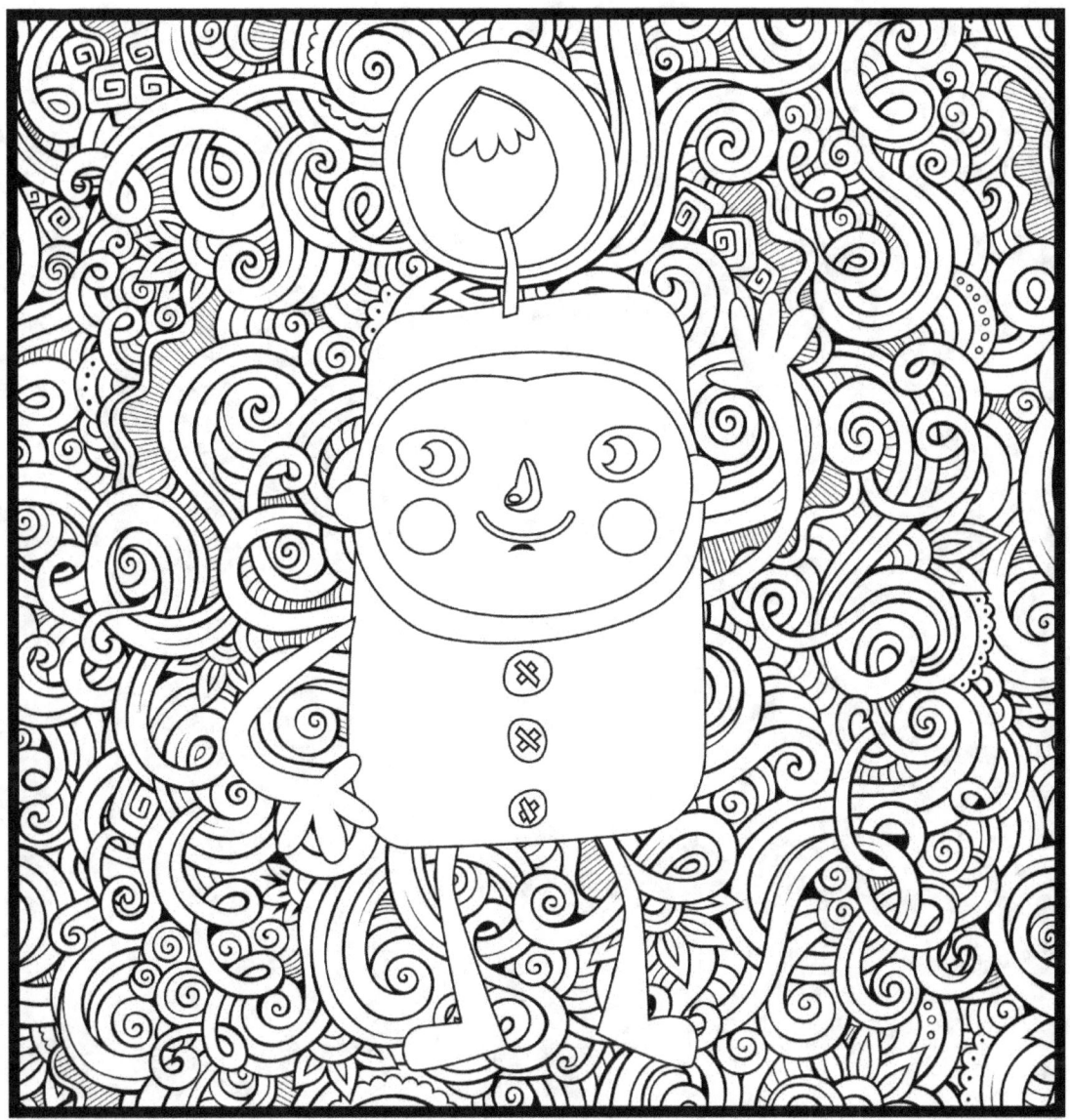

note:

_____

_____

_____

DECEMBER 11TH

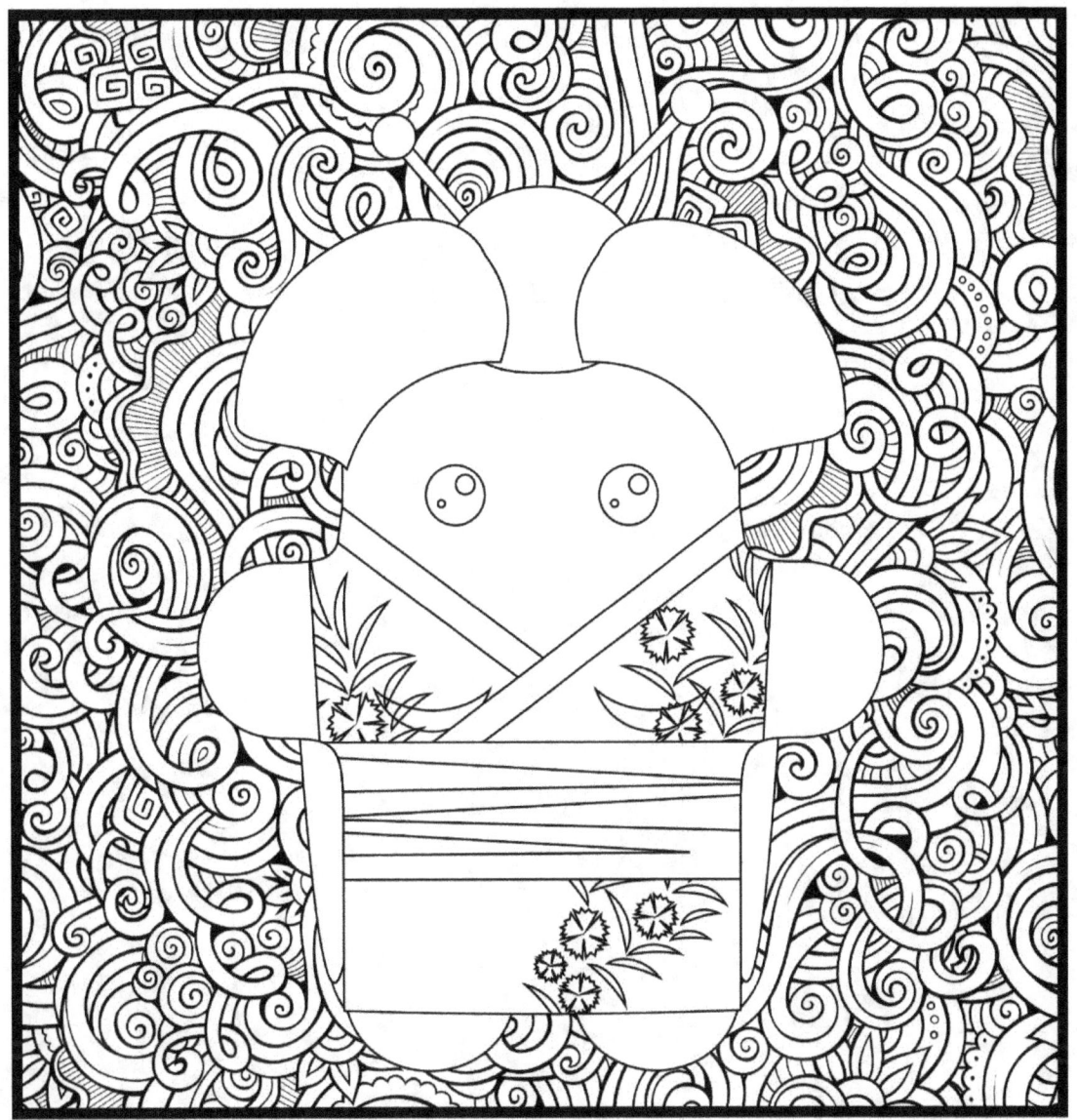

note:

_____

_____

_____

DECEMBER 12TH

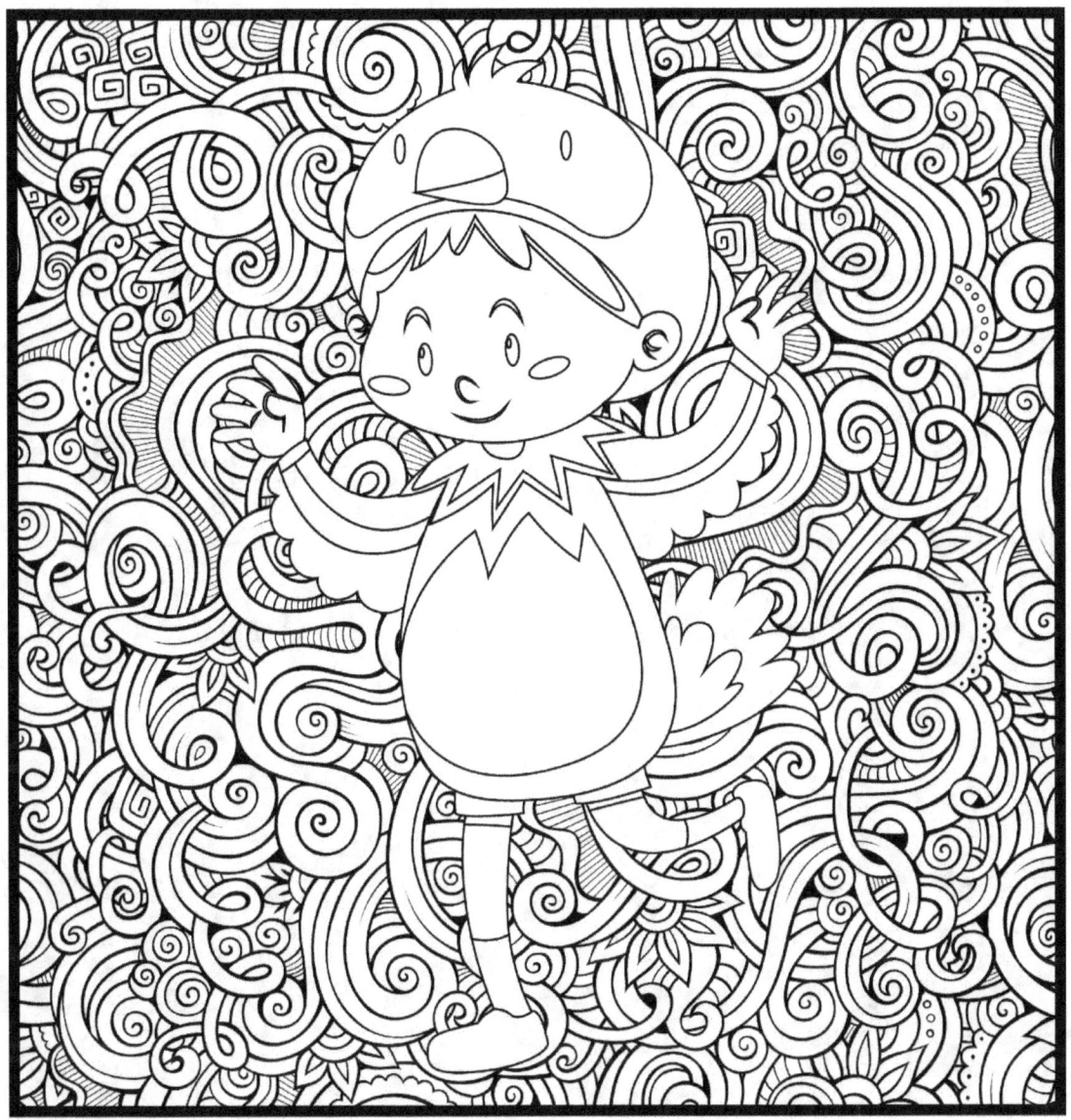

note:

_____

_____

_____

DECEMBER 13TH

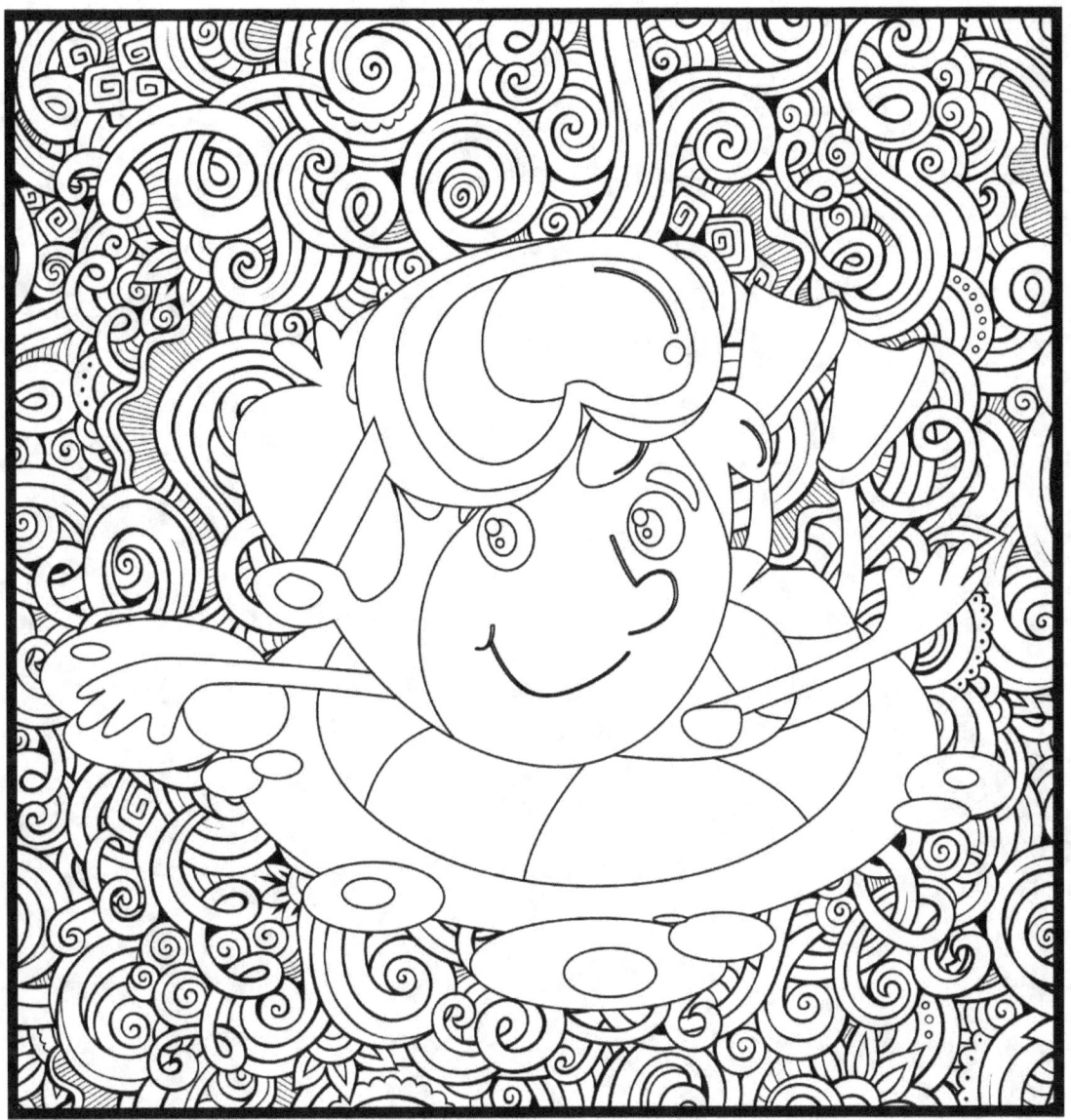

note:

_____

_____

_____

DECEMBER 14TH

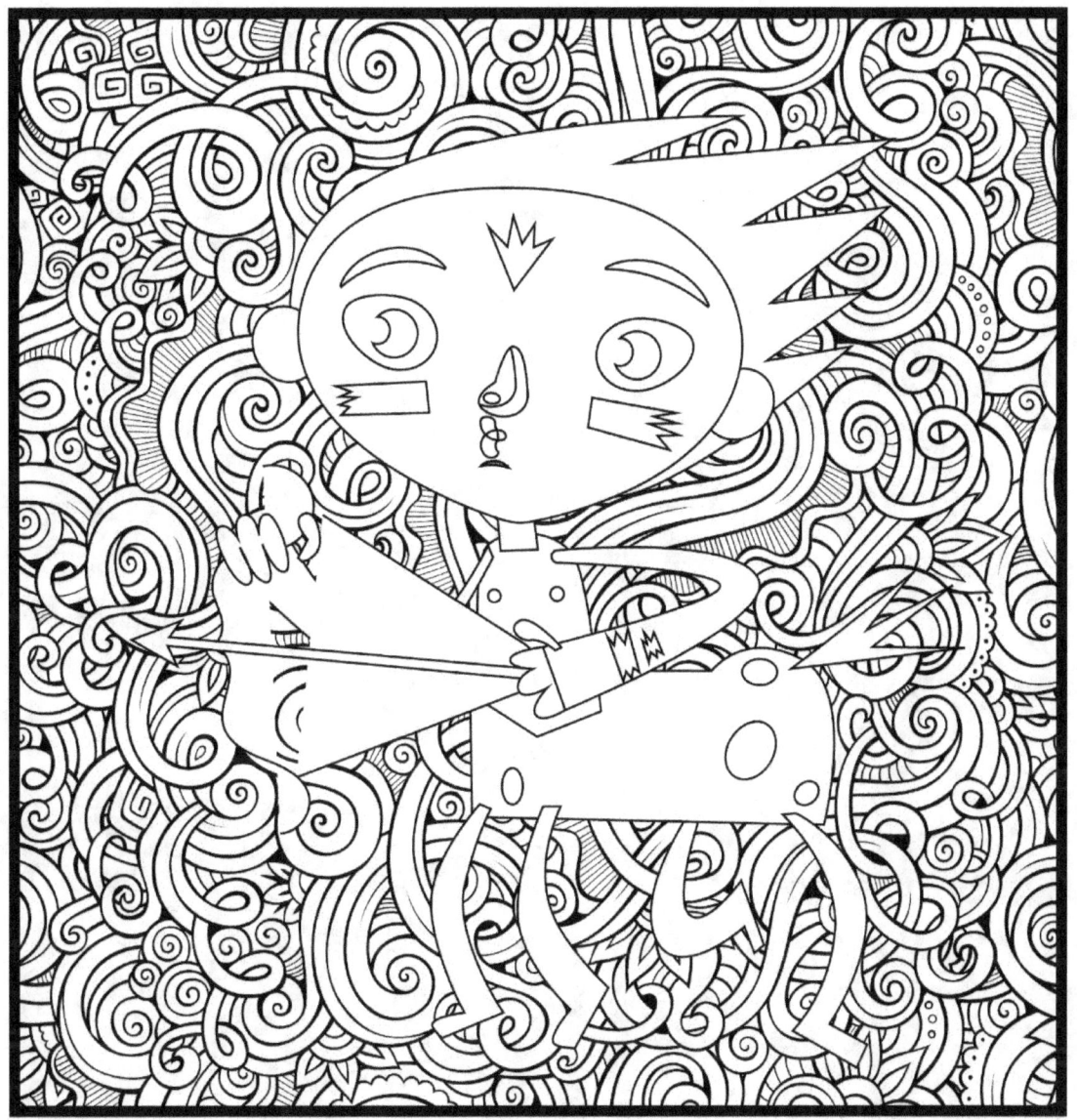

note:

_____

_____

_____

DECEMBER 15TH

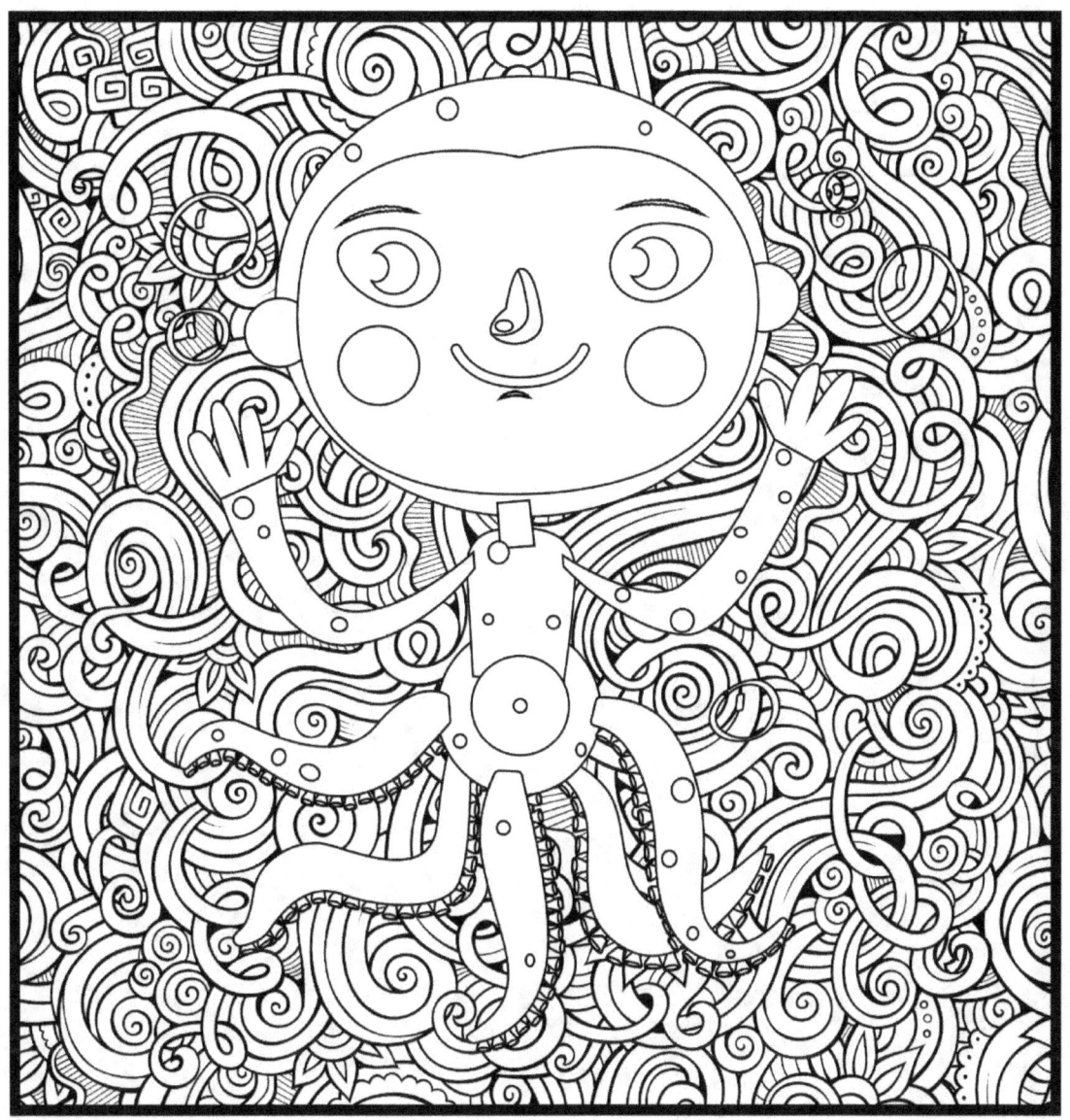

note:

_____

_____

_____

DECEMBER 16TH

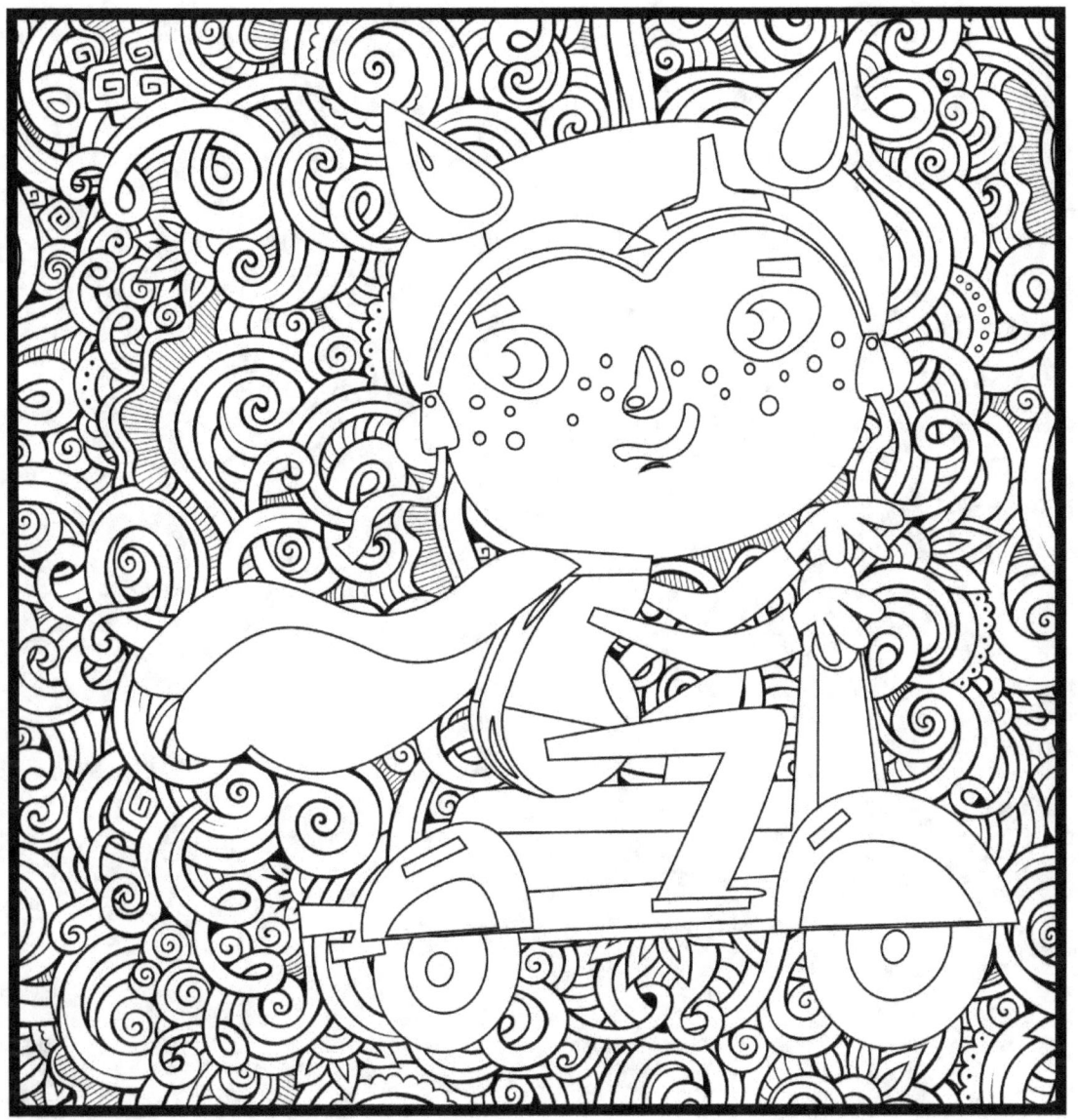

note:

_____

_____

_____

DECEMBER 17TH

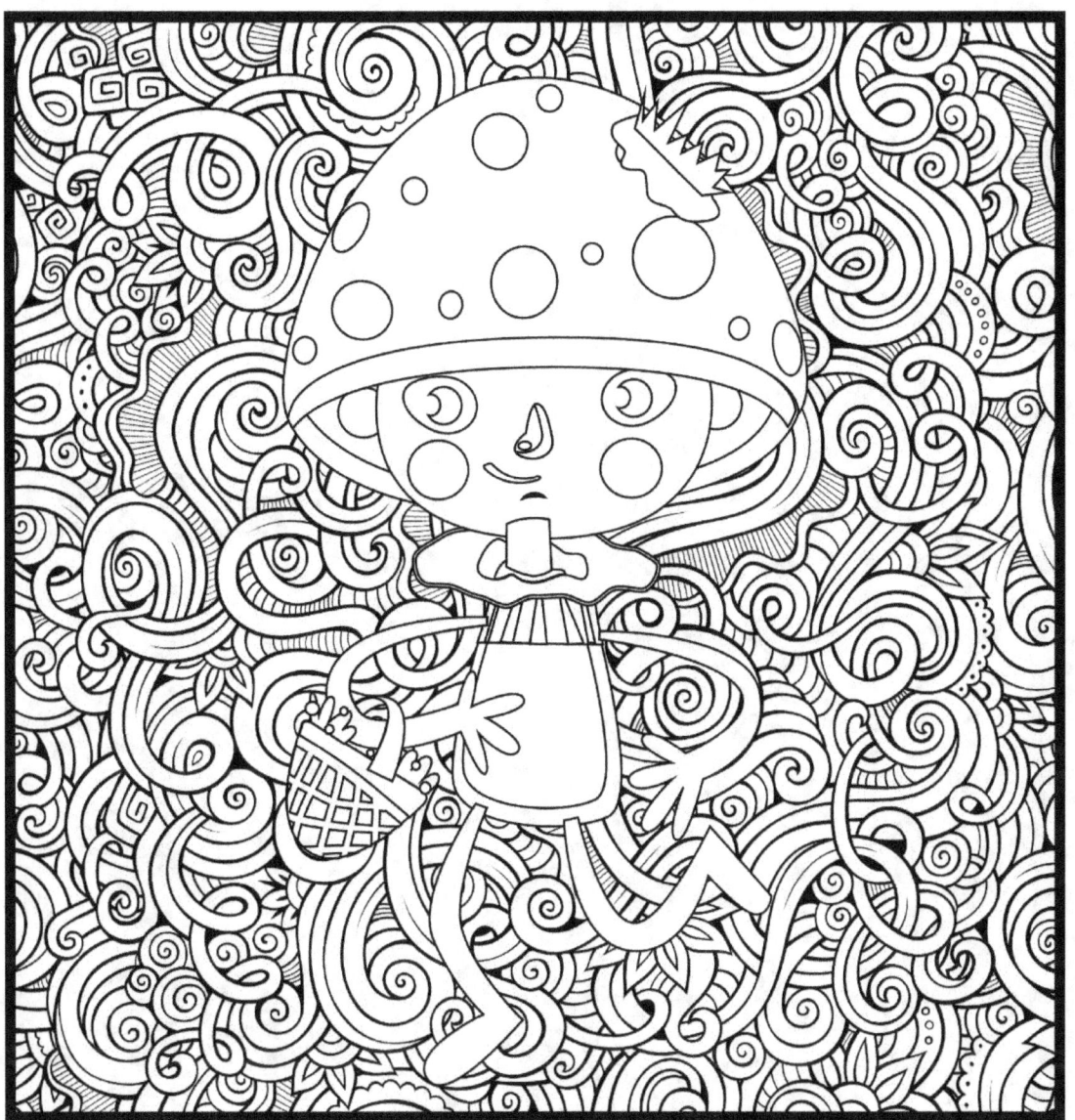

note:

_____

_____

_____

DECEMBER 18TH

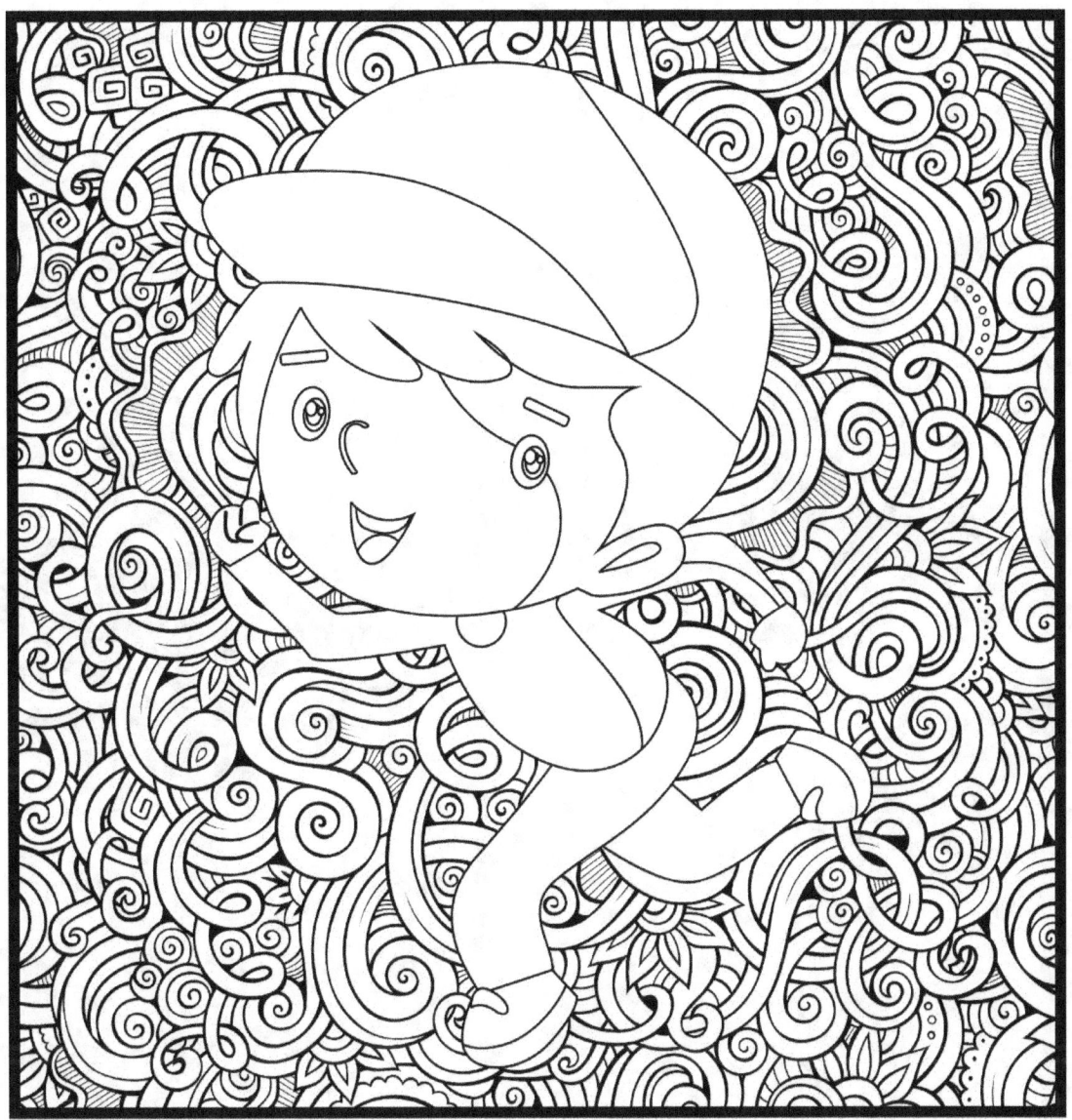

note:

_____

_____

_____

DECEMBER 19TH

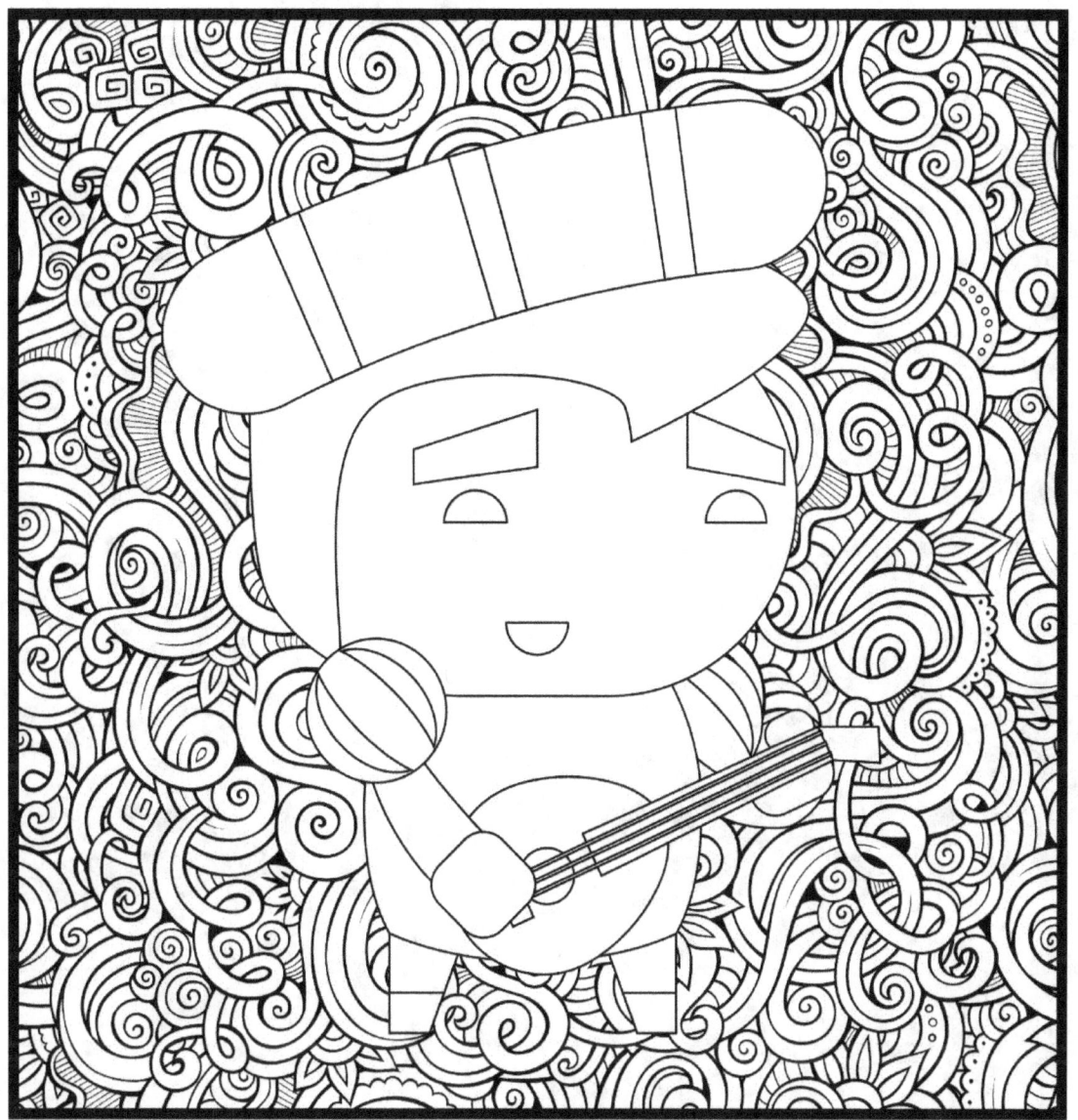

note:

_____

_____

_____

DECEMBER 20TH

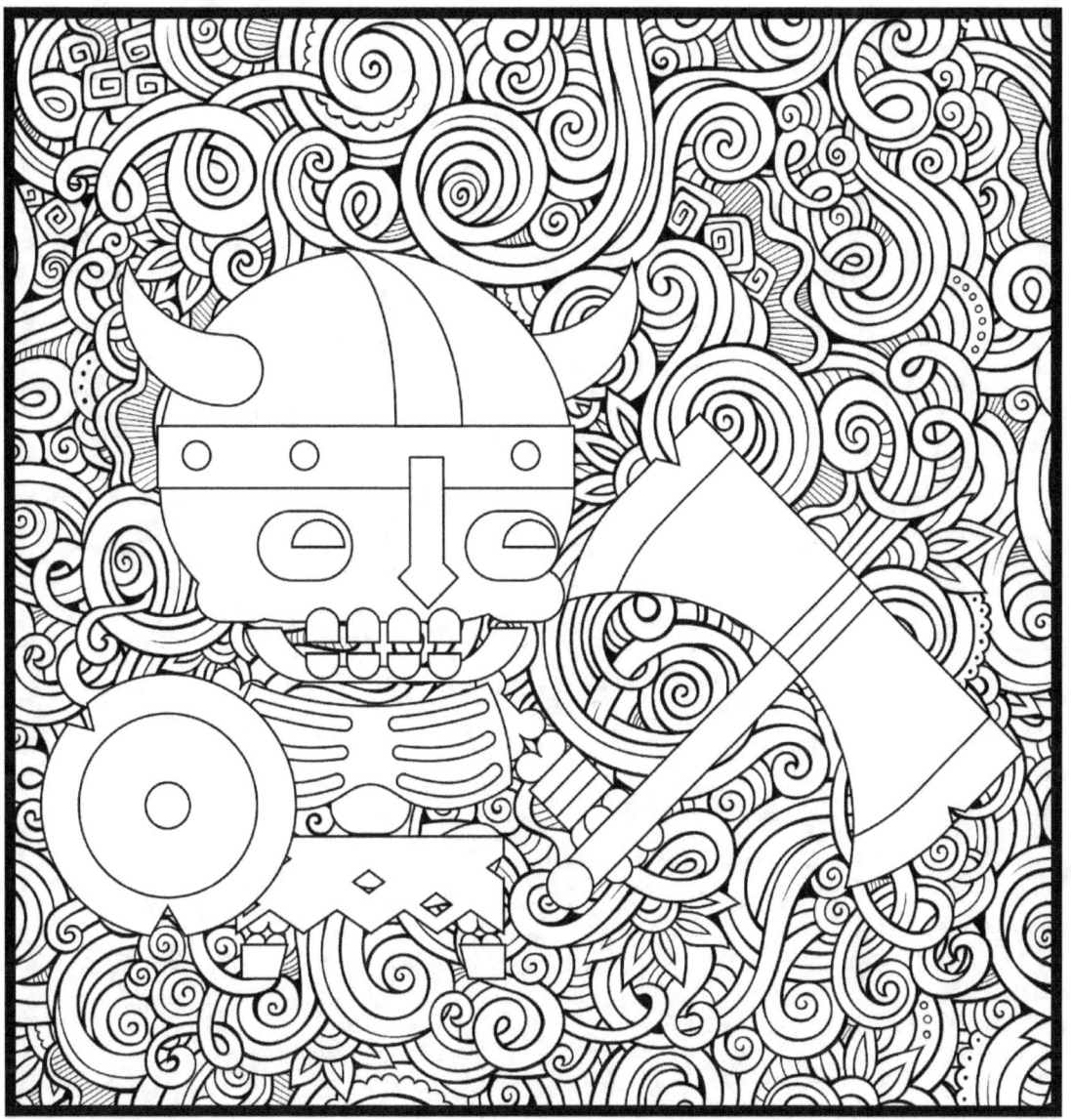

note:

_____

_____

_____

DECEMBER 21TH

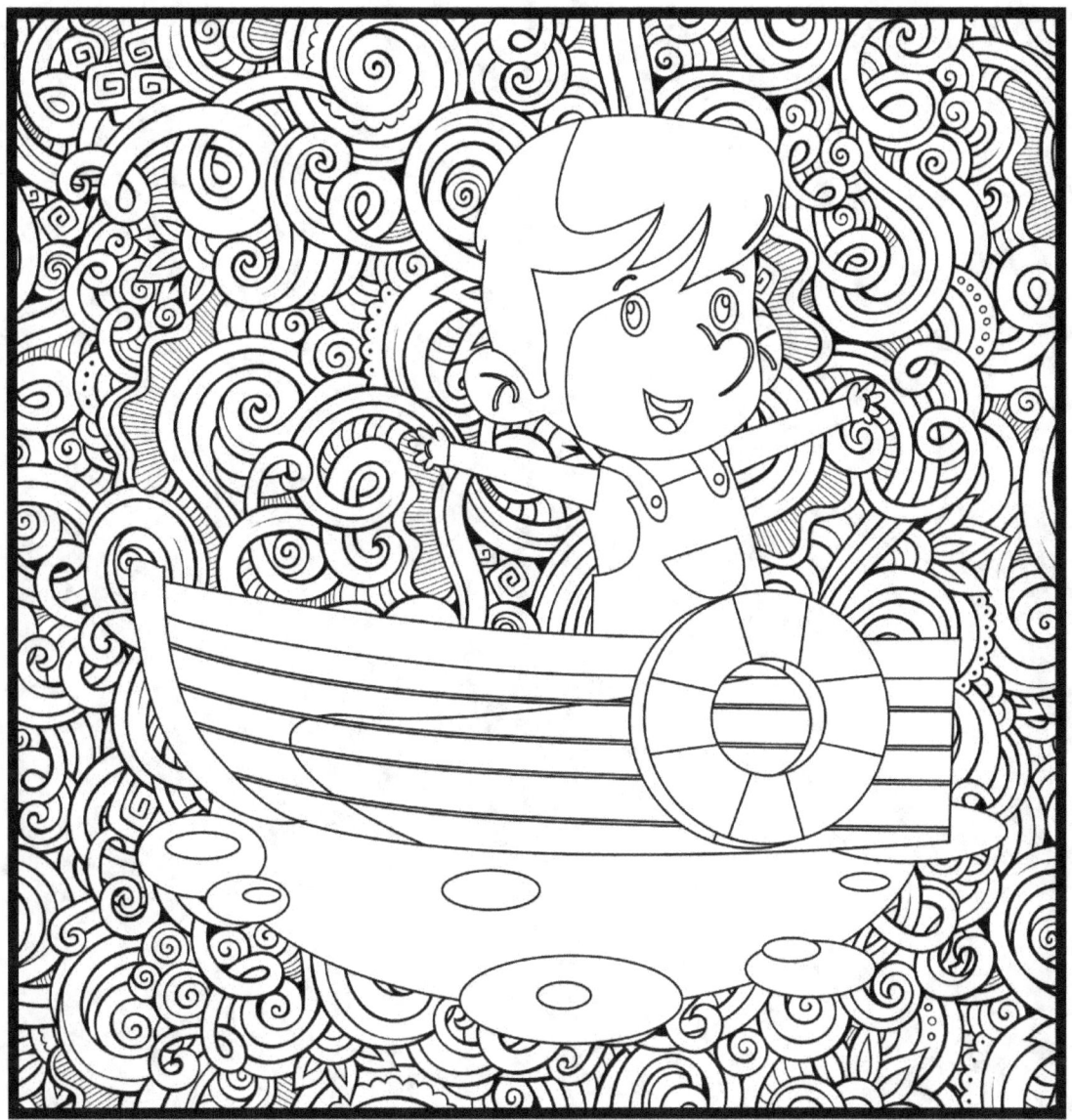

note:

_____

_____

_____

DECEMBER 22TH

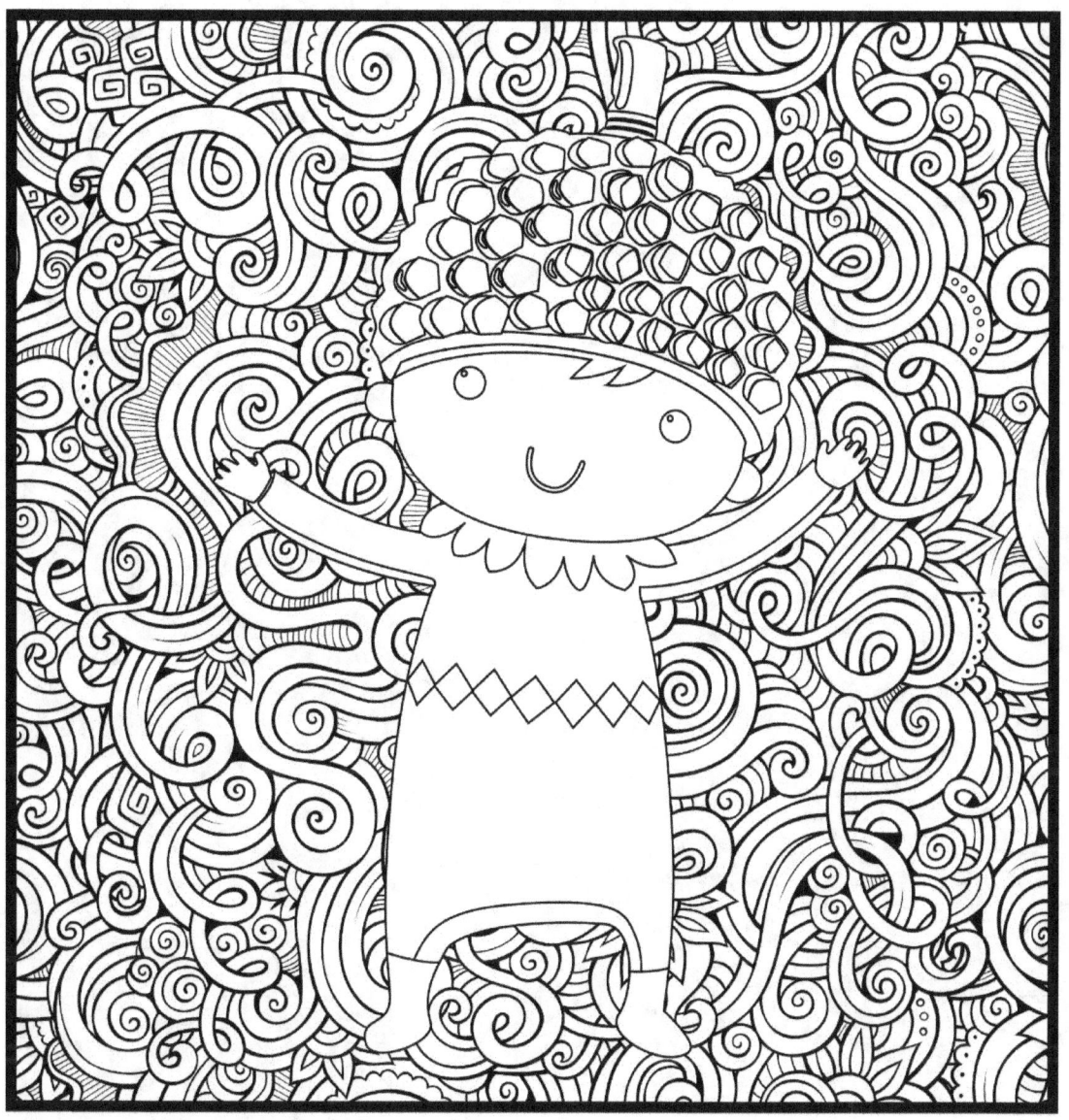

note:

_____

_____

_____

DECEMBER 23TH

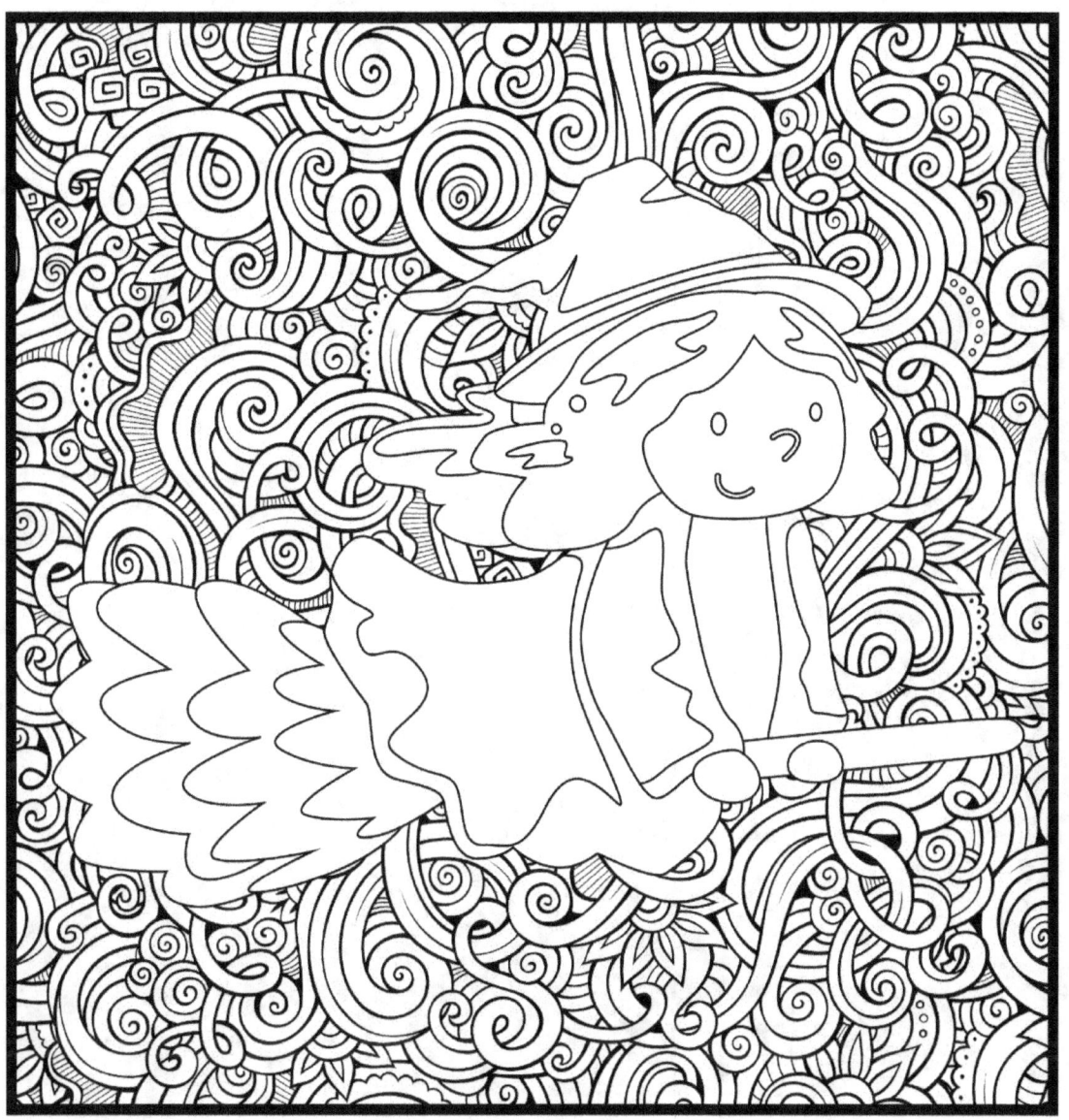

note:

_____

_____

_____

DECEMBER 24TH

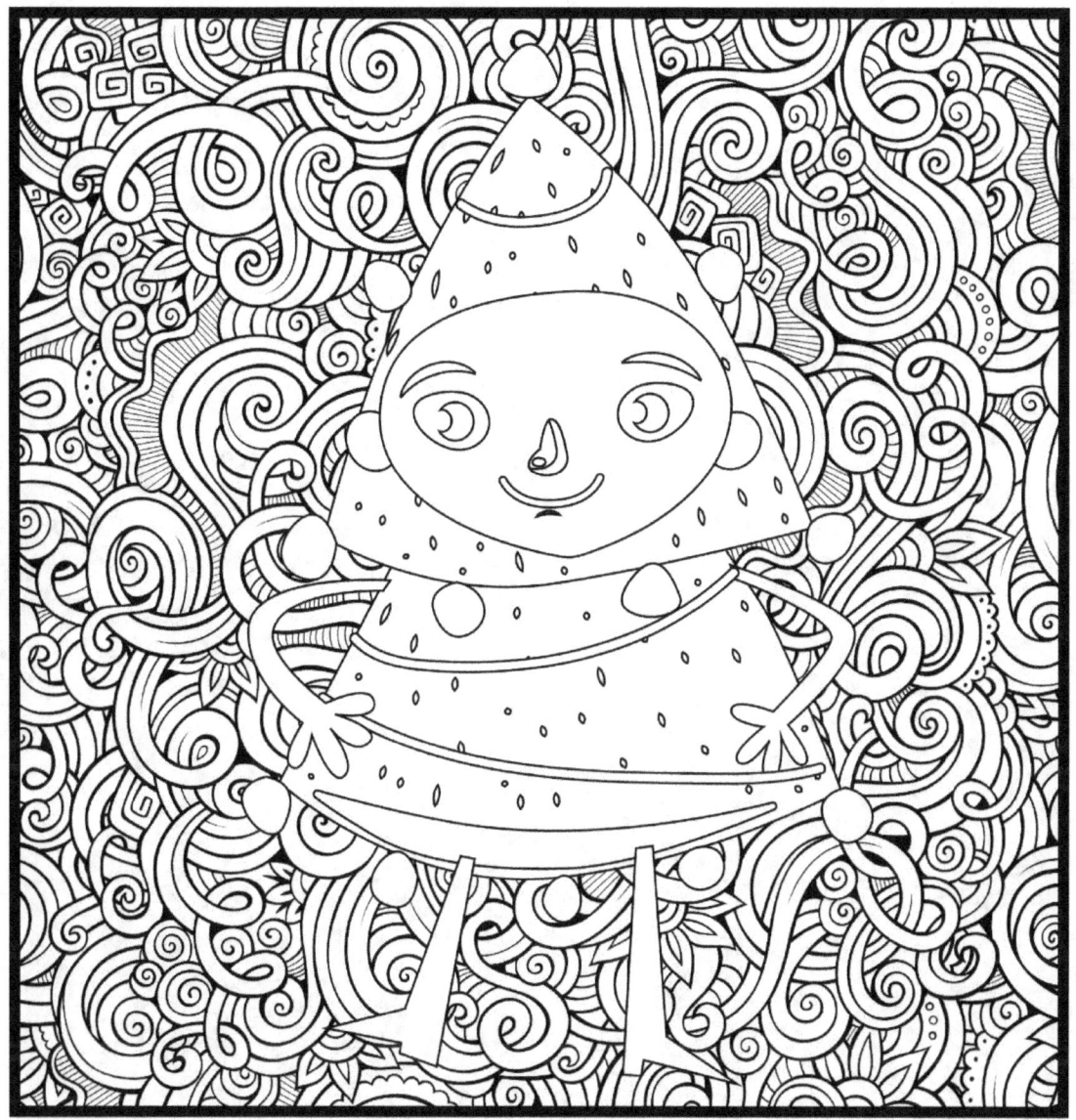

note:

_____

_____

_____

DECEMBER 25TH

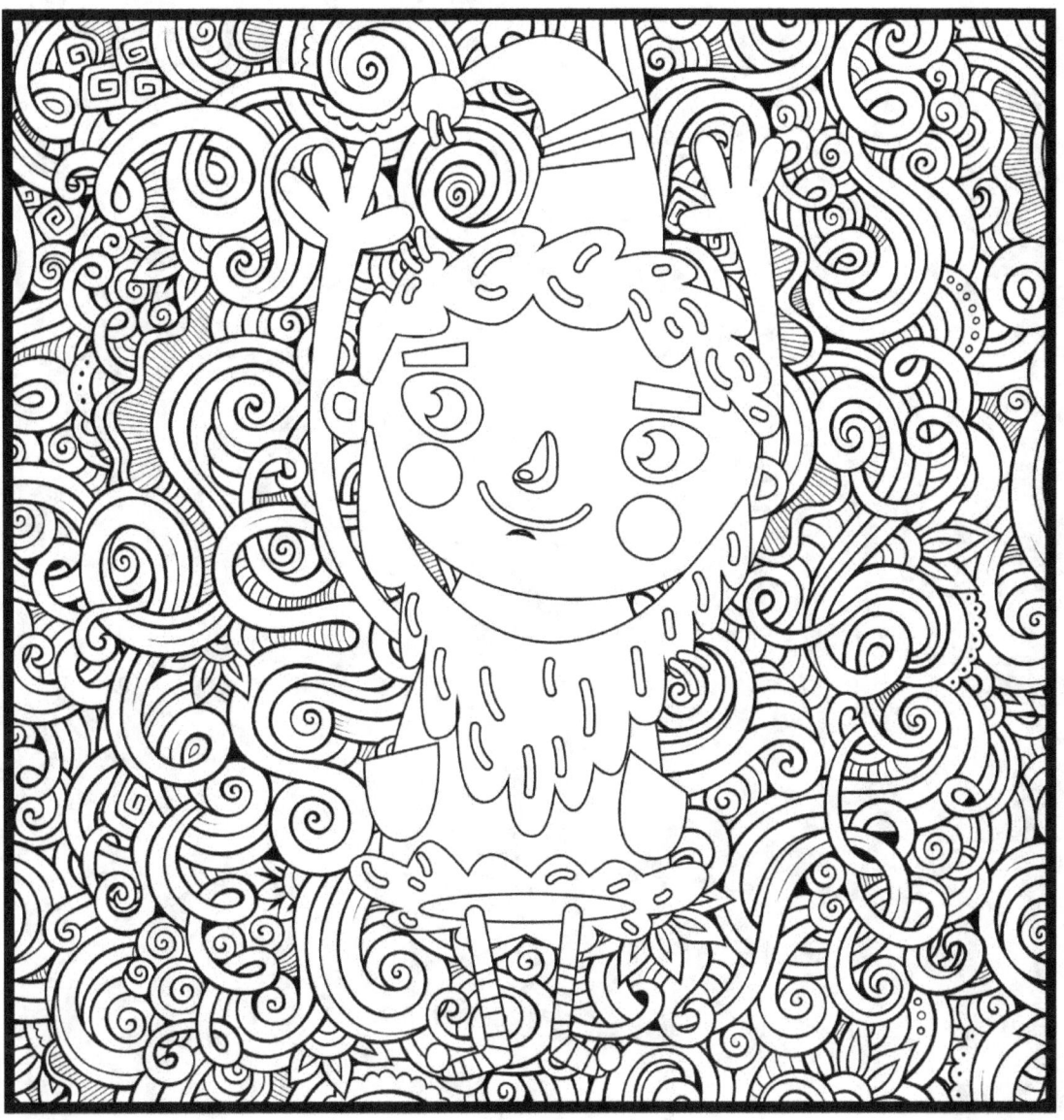

note:

_____

_____

_____

DECEMBER 26TH

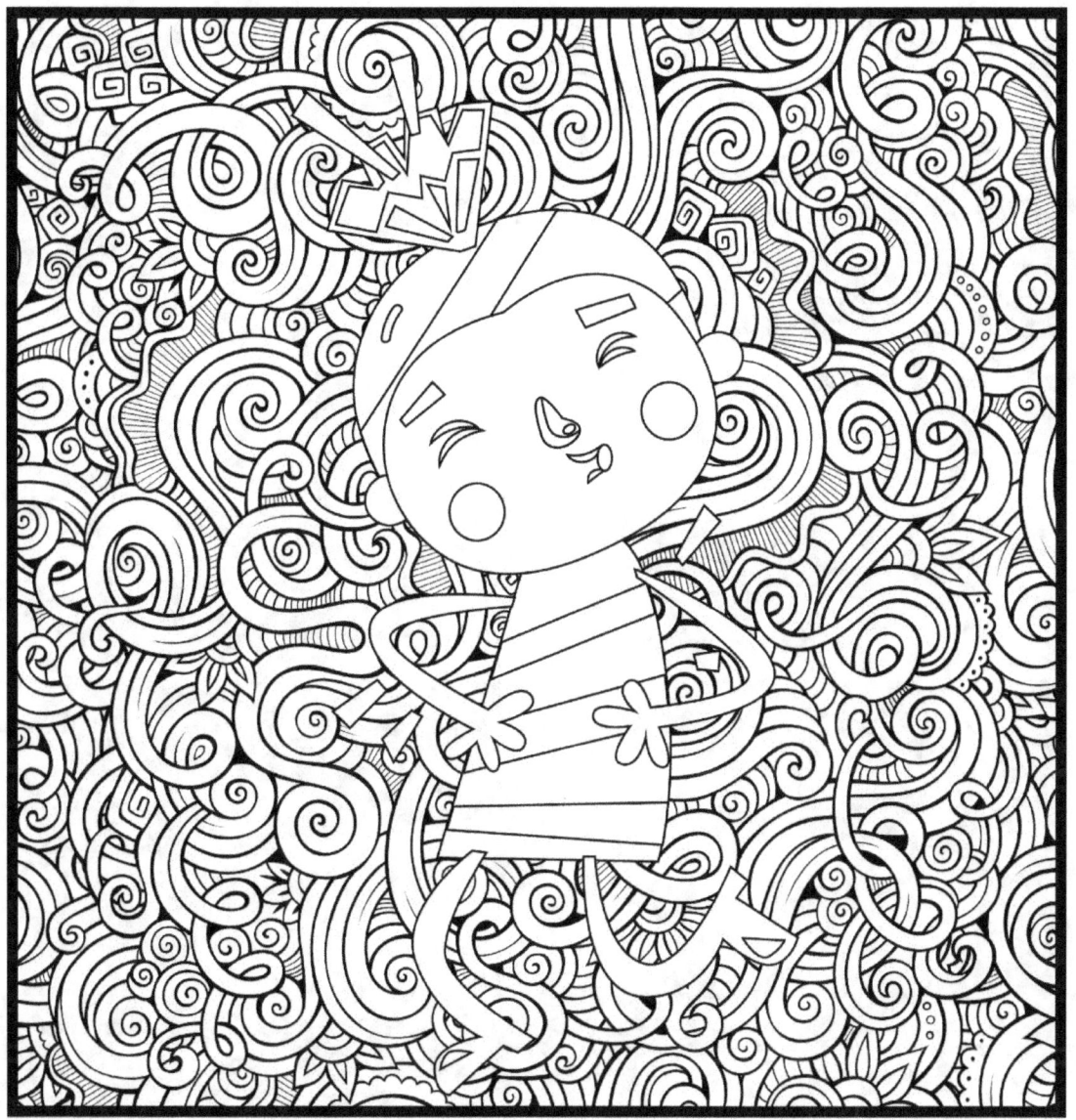

note:

_____

_____

_____

DECEMBER 27TH

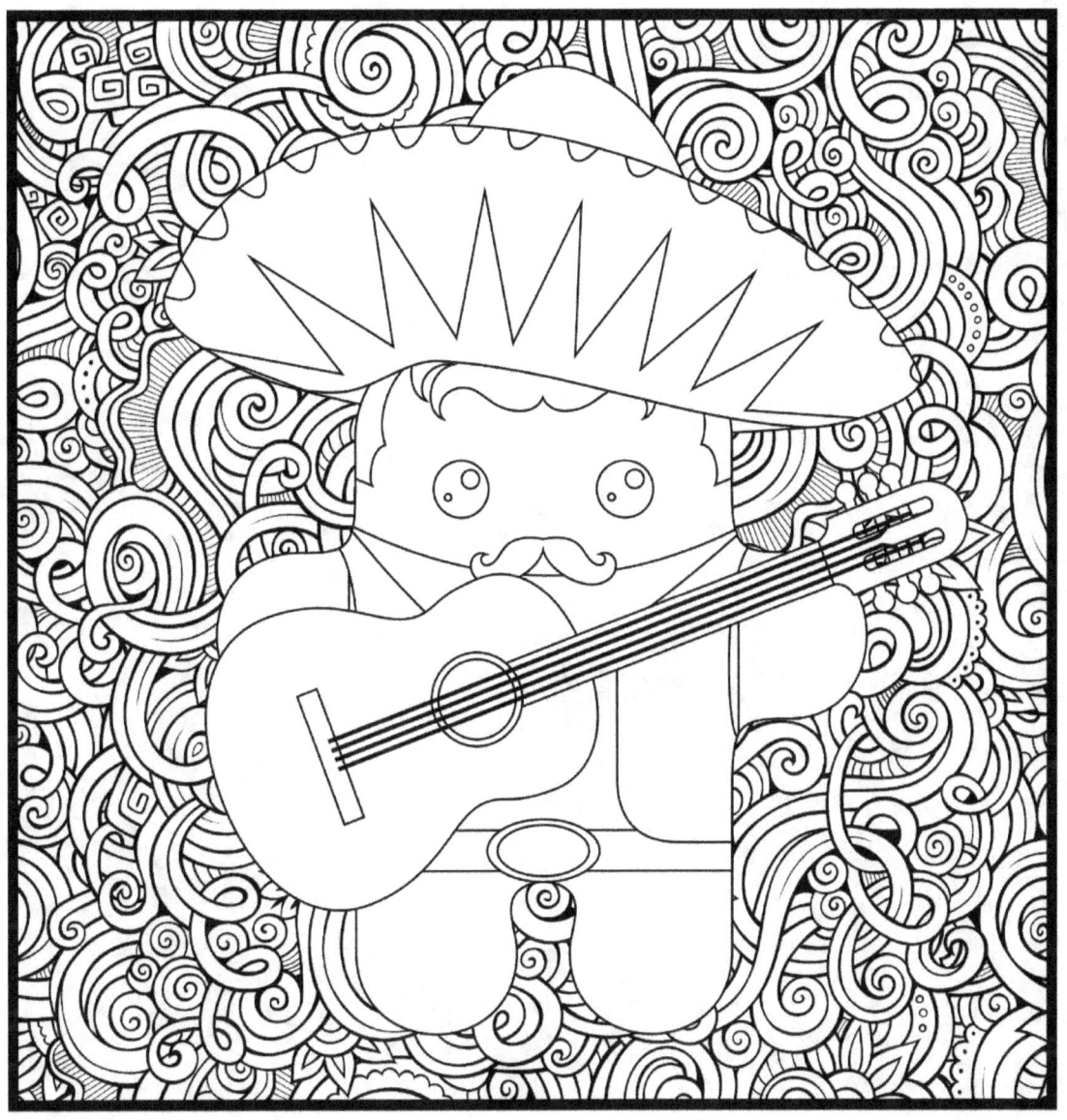

note:

_____

_____

_____

DECEMBER 28TH

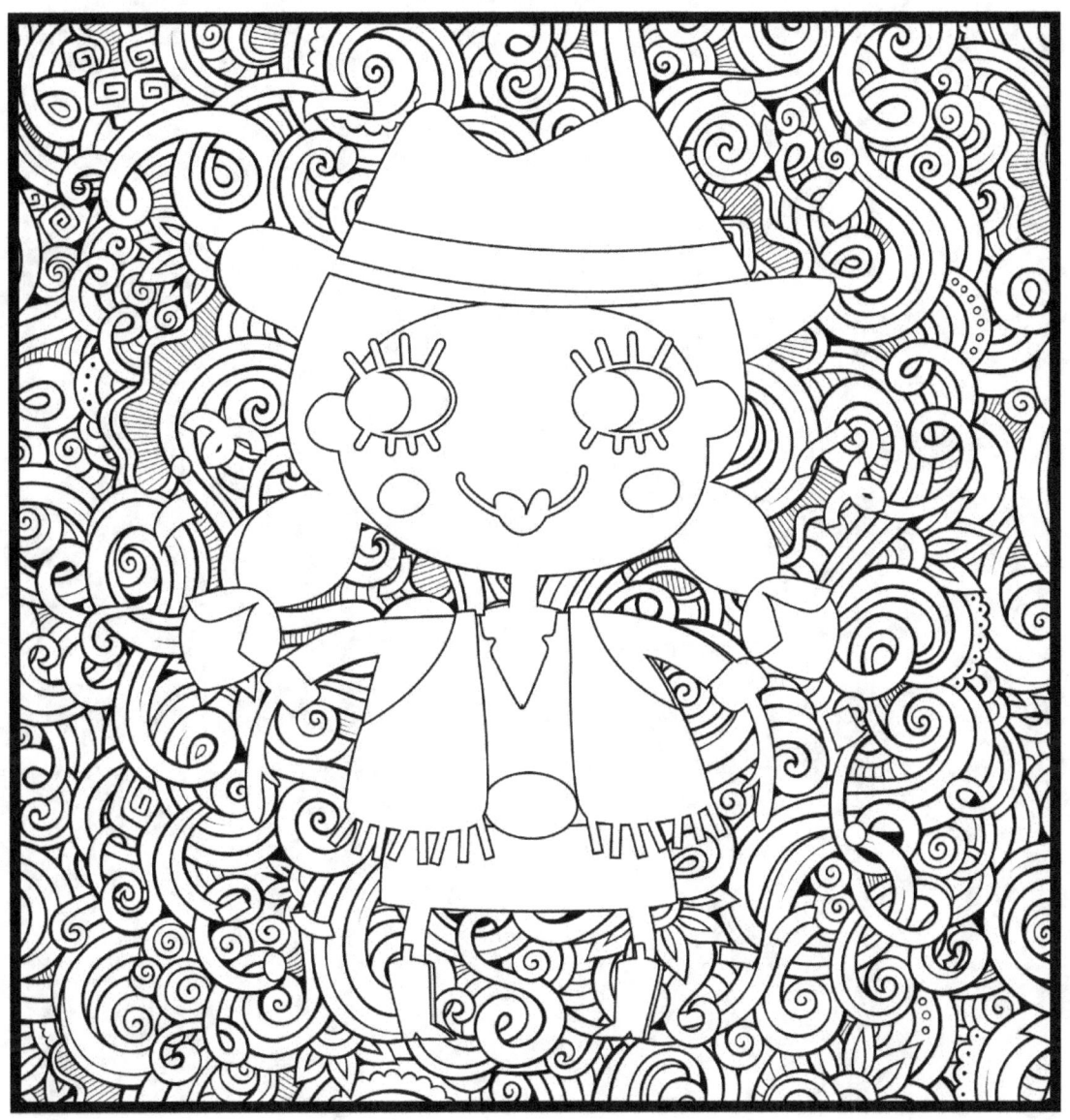

note:

_____

_____

_____

DECEMBER 29TH

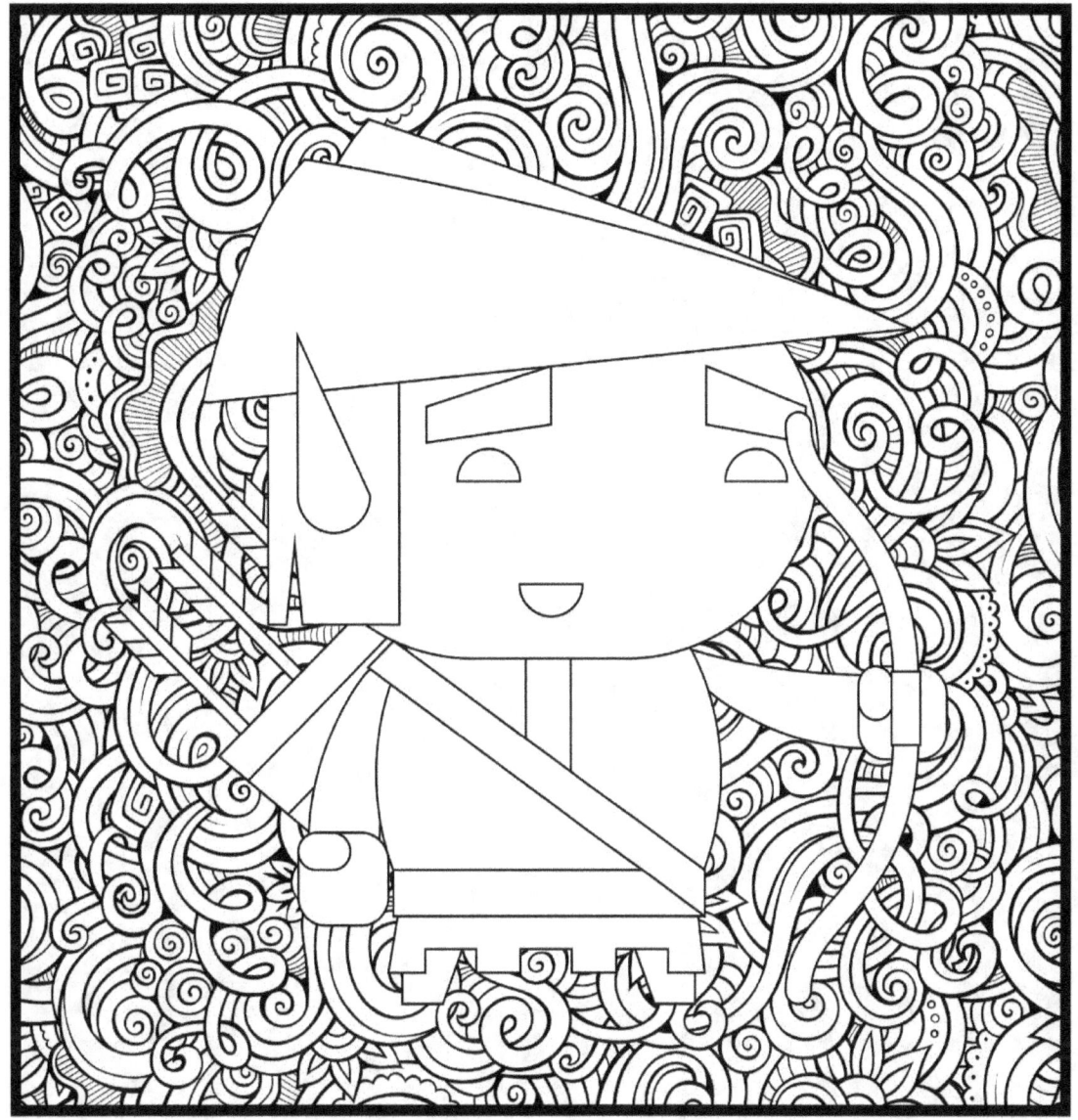

note:

_____

_____

_____

DECEMBER 30TH

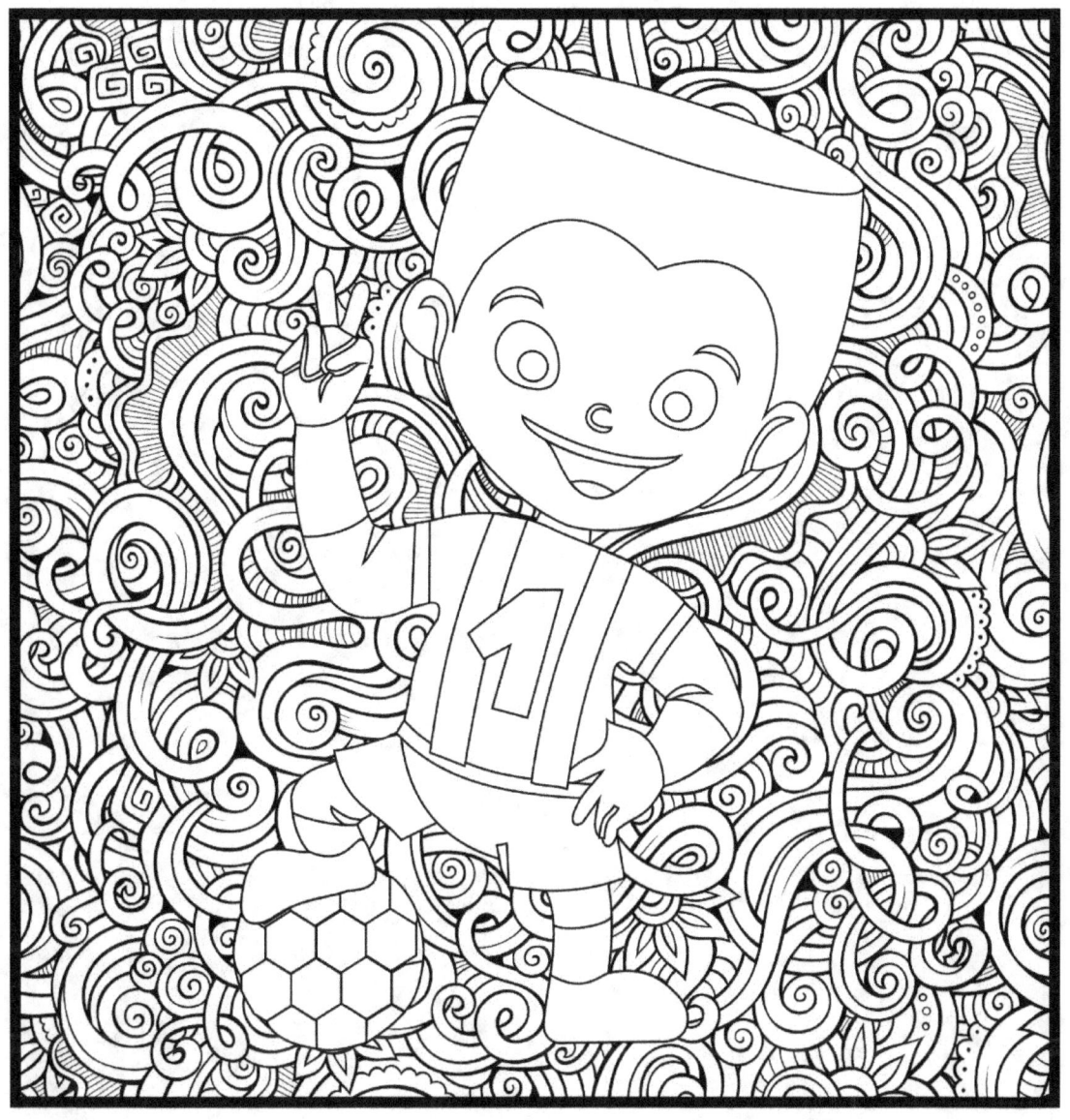

note:

_____

_____

_____

DECEMBER 31TH

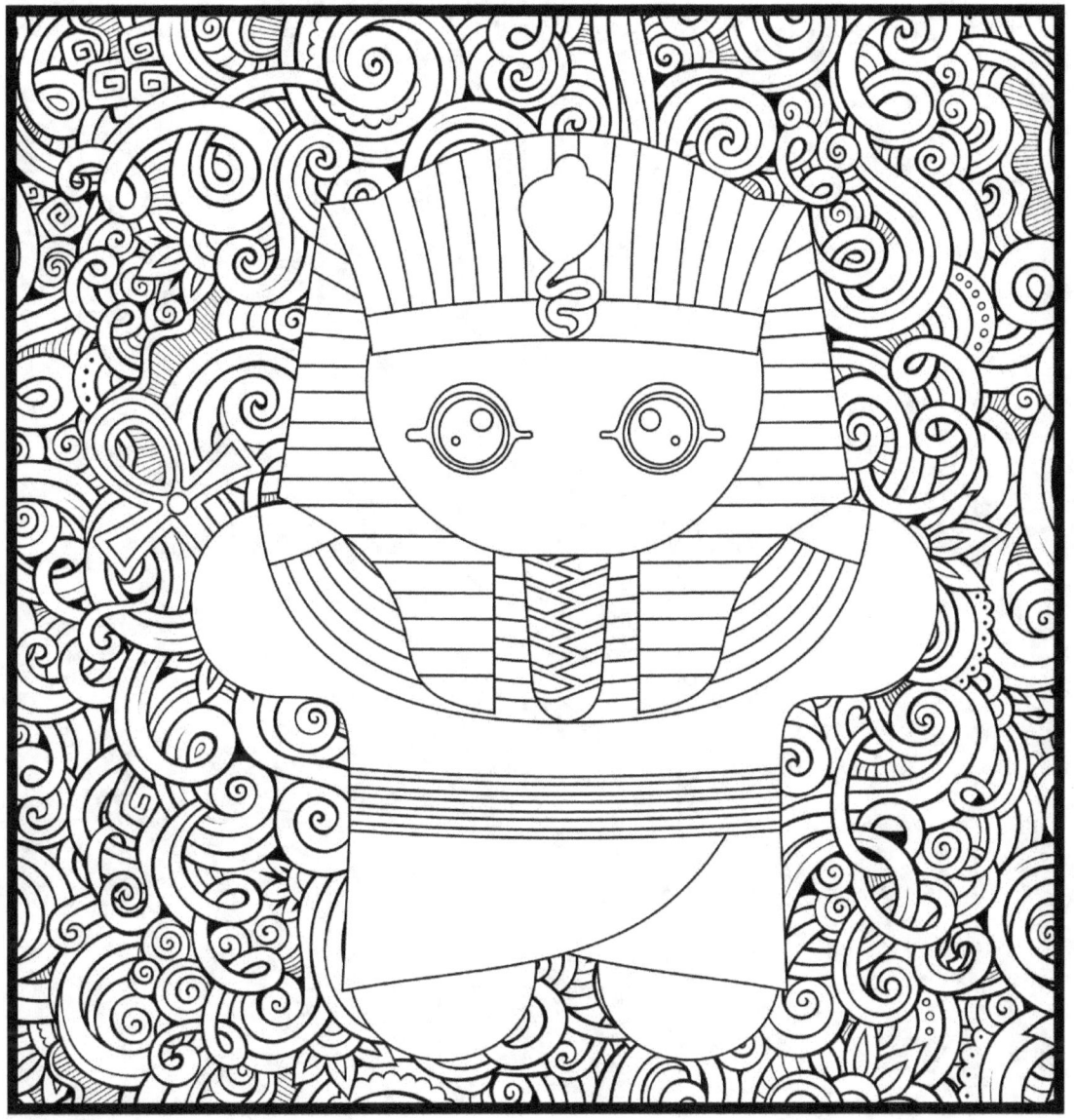

note:

_____

_____

_____

DECEMBER 32TH

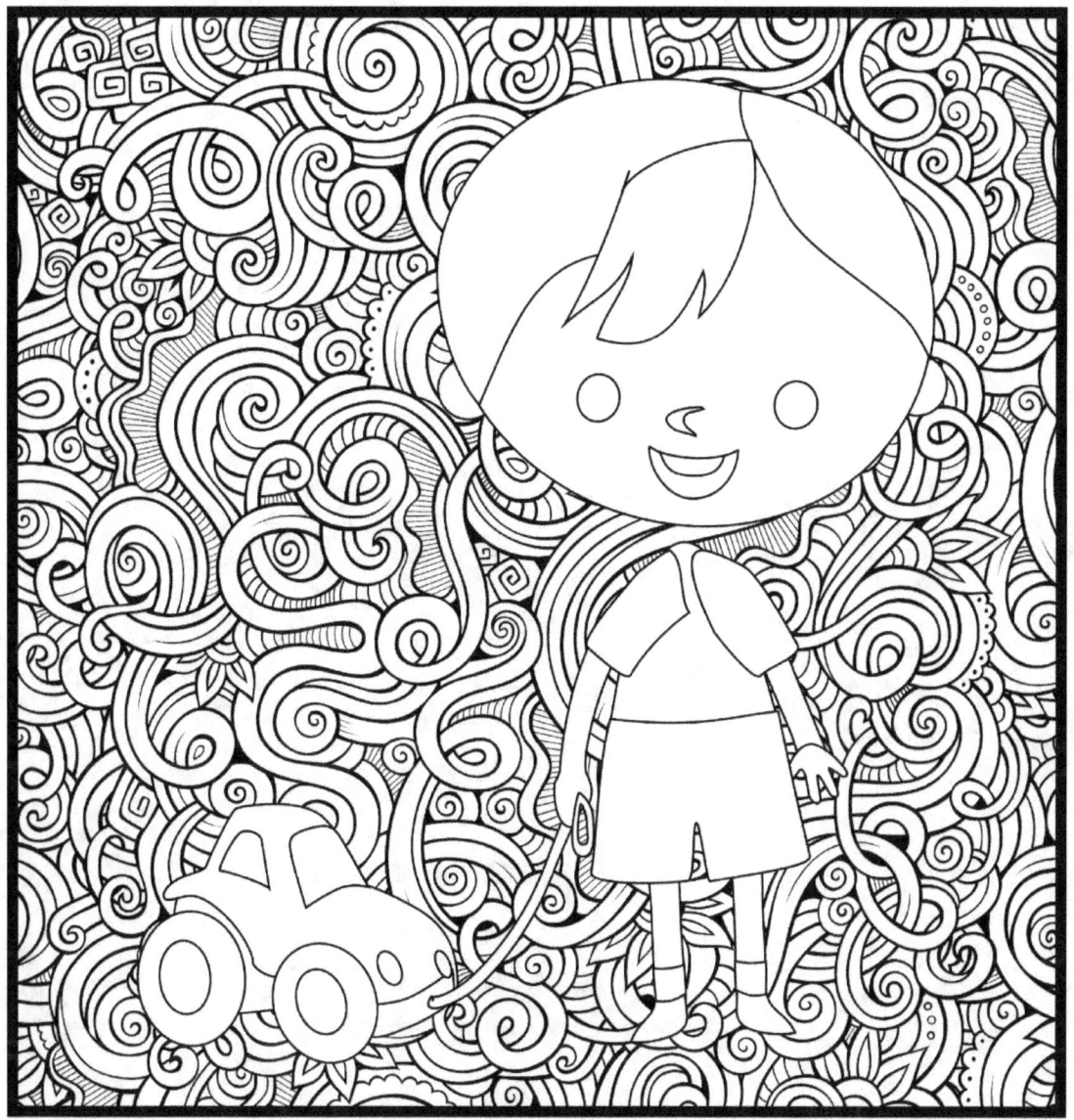

note:

_____

_____

_____

DECEMBER 33TH

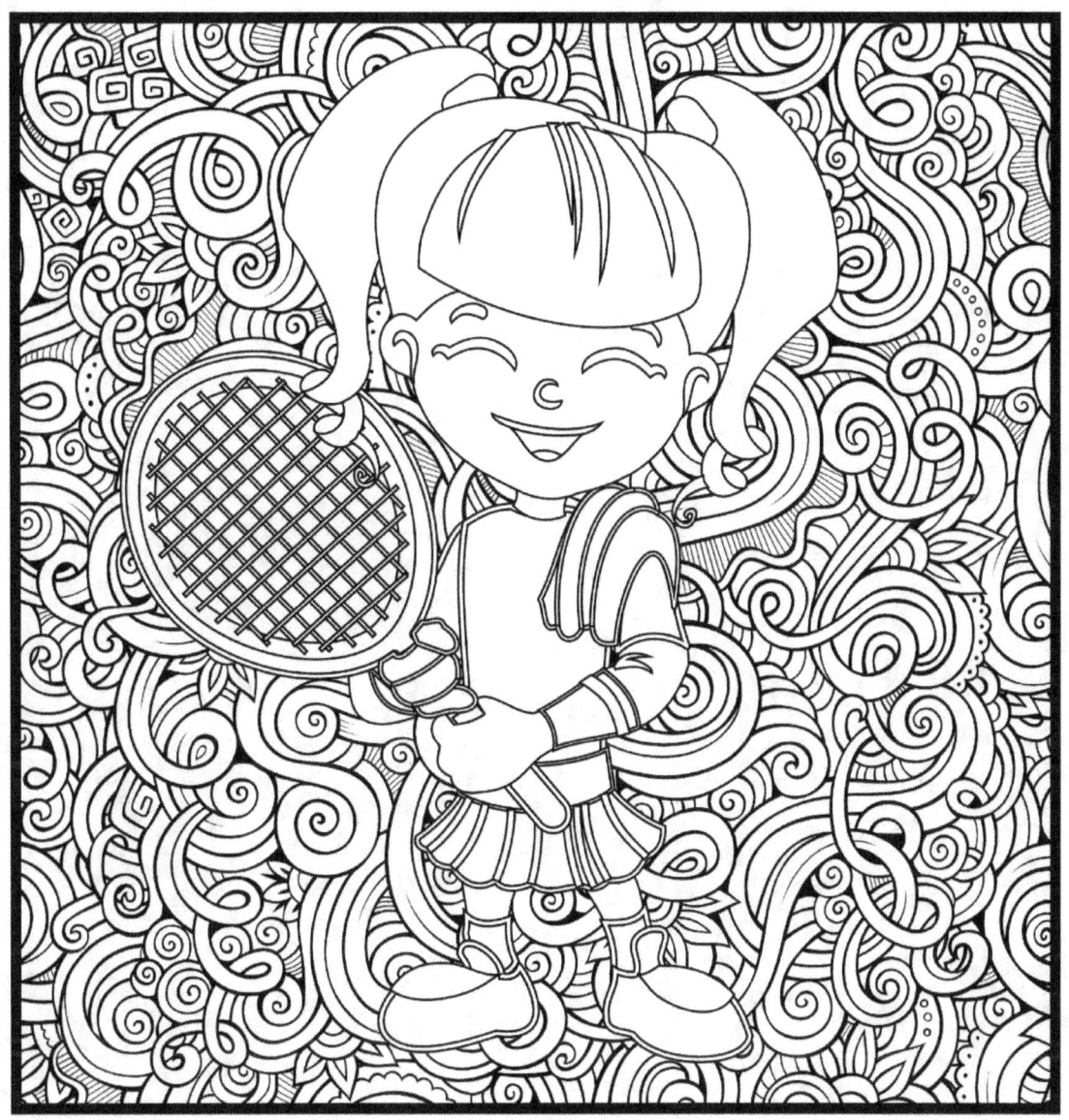

note:

_____

_____

_____

DECEMBER 34TH

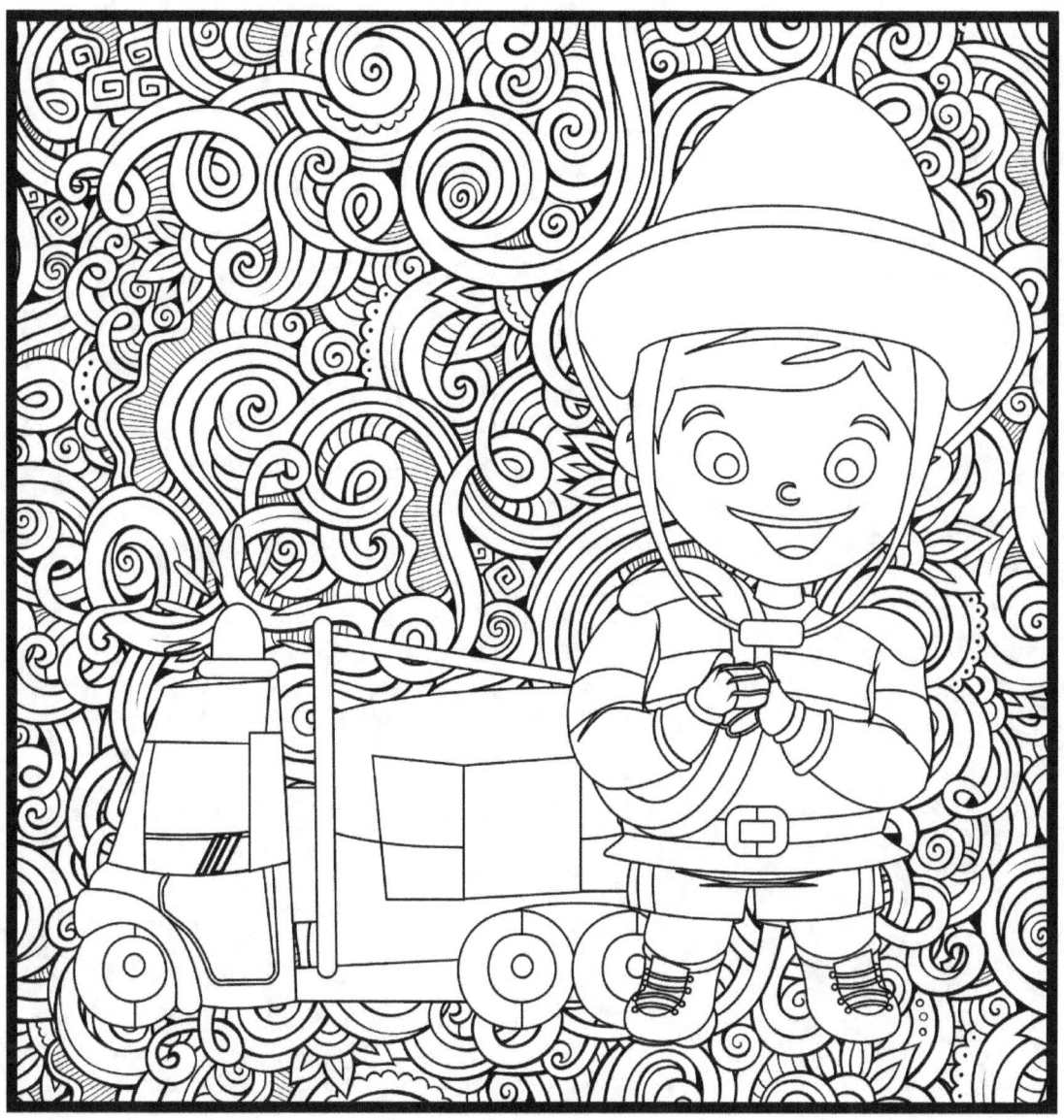

note:

_____

_____

_____

DECEMBER 35TH

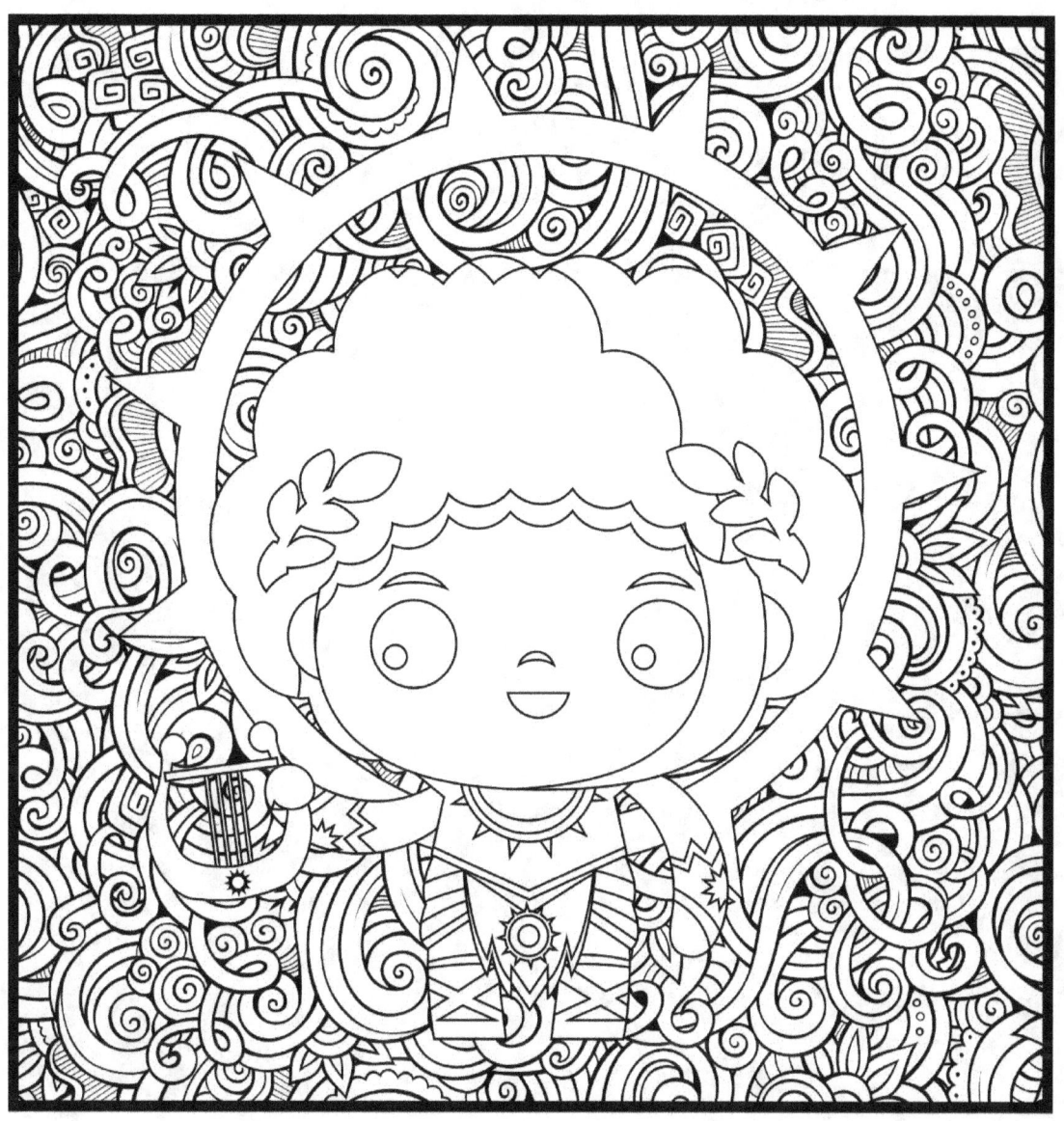

note:

_____

_____

_____

DECEMBER 36TH

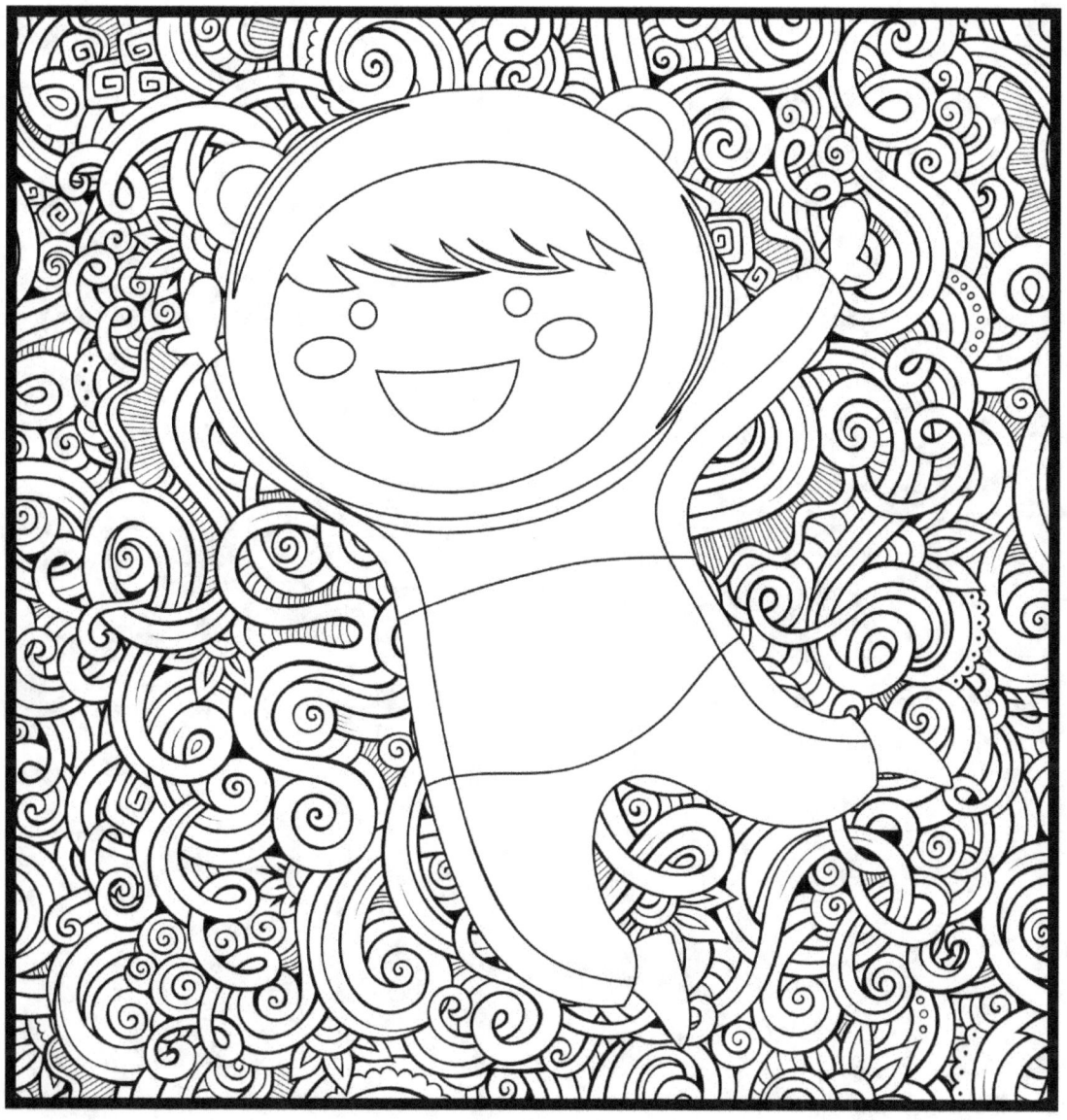

note:

_____

_____

_____

DECEMBER 37TH

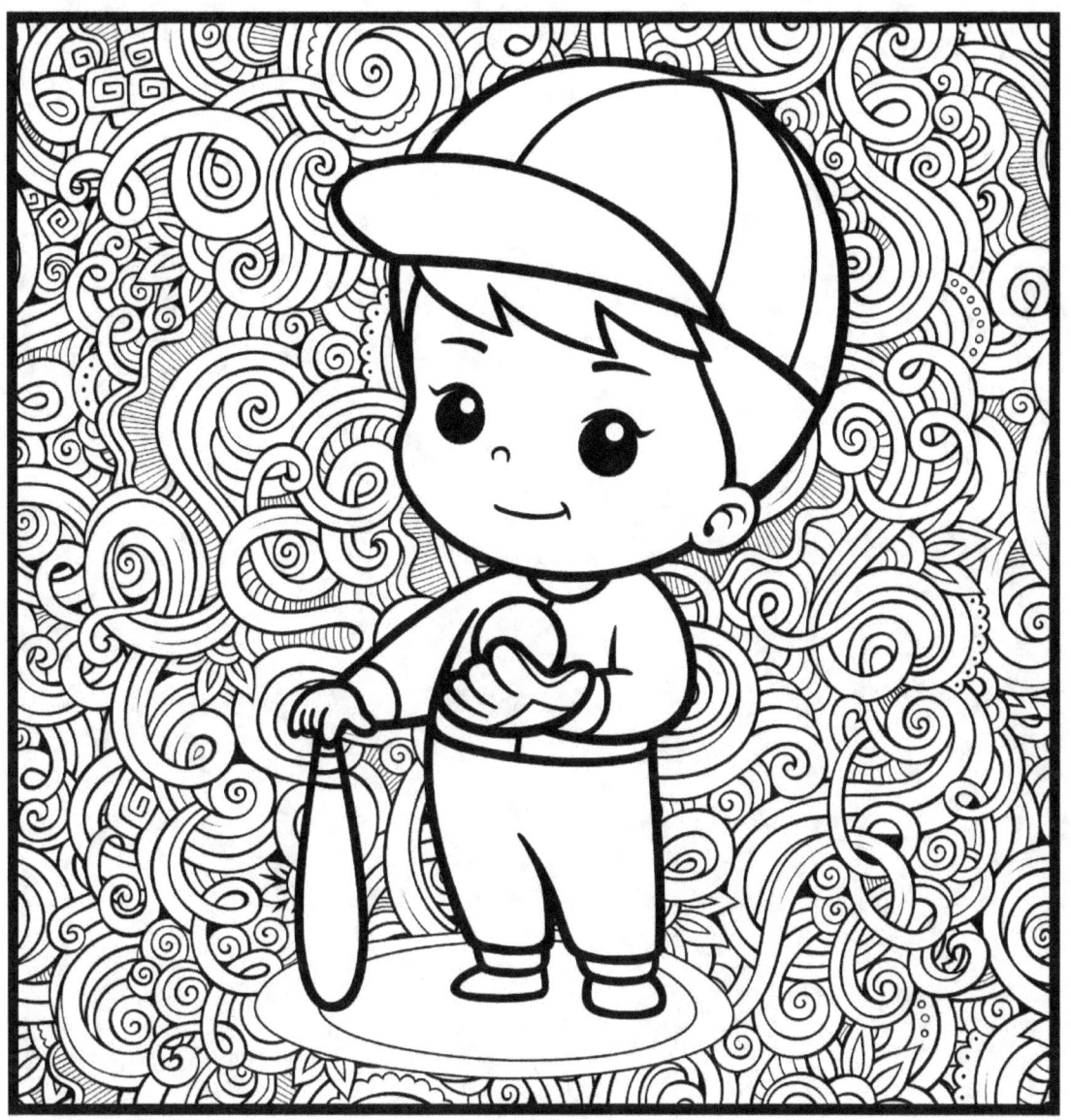

note:

_____

_____

_____

DECEMBER 38TH

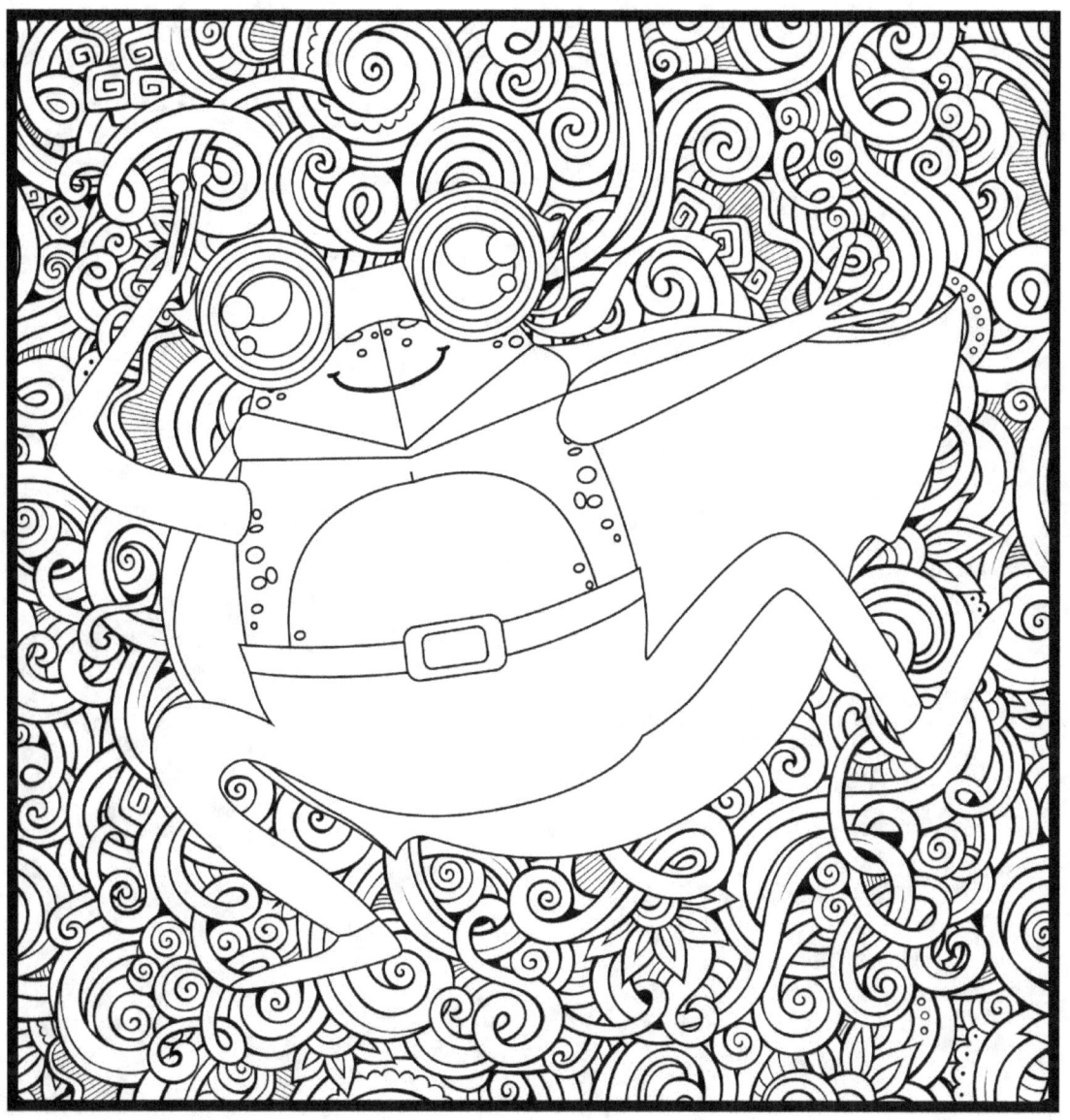

note:

_____

_____

_____

DECEMBER 39TH

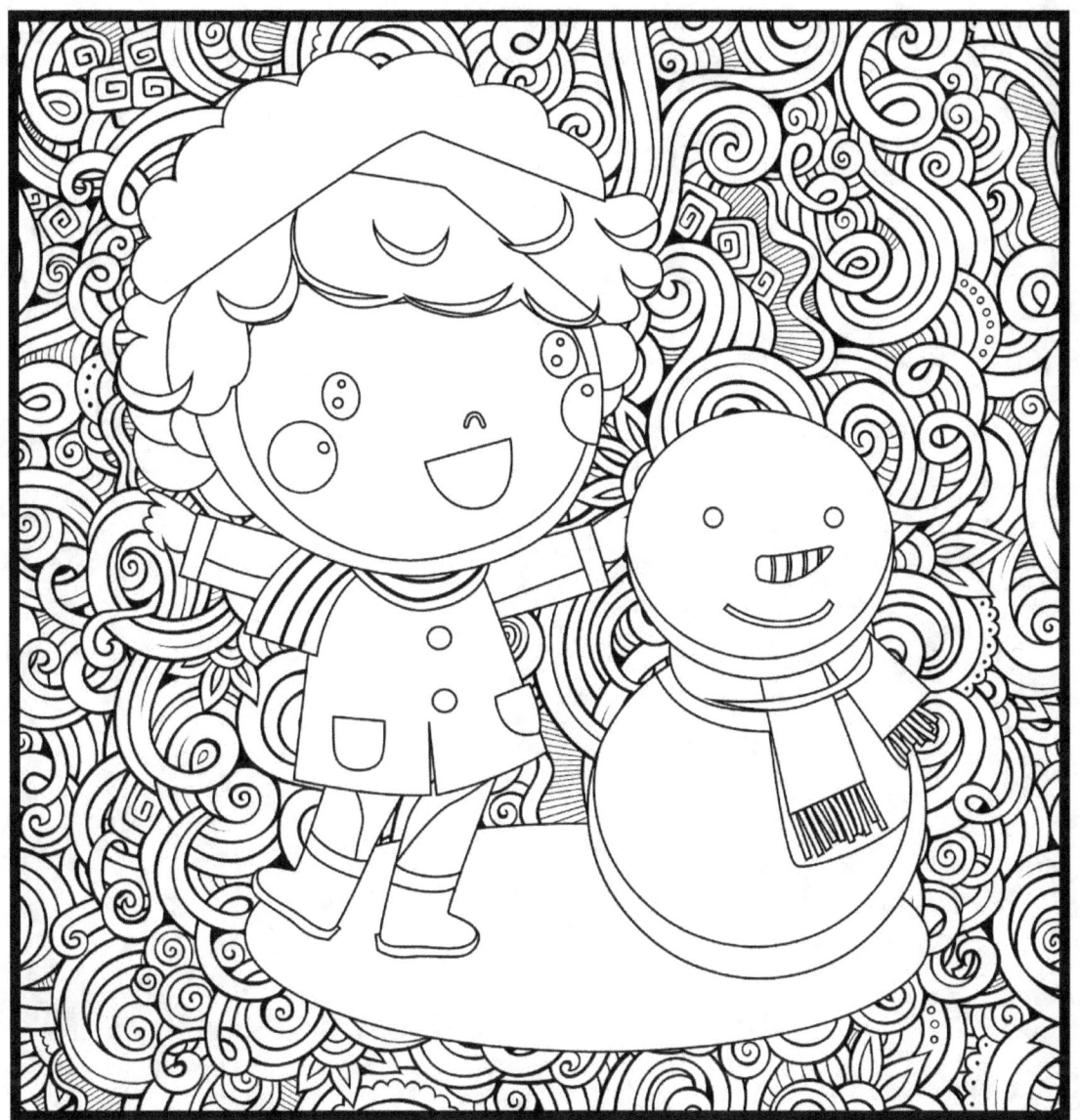

note:

_____

_____

_____

DECEMBER 40TH

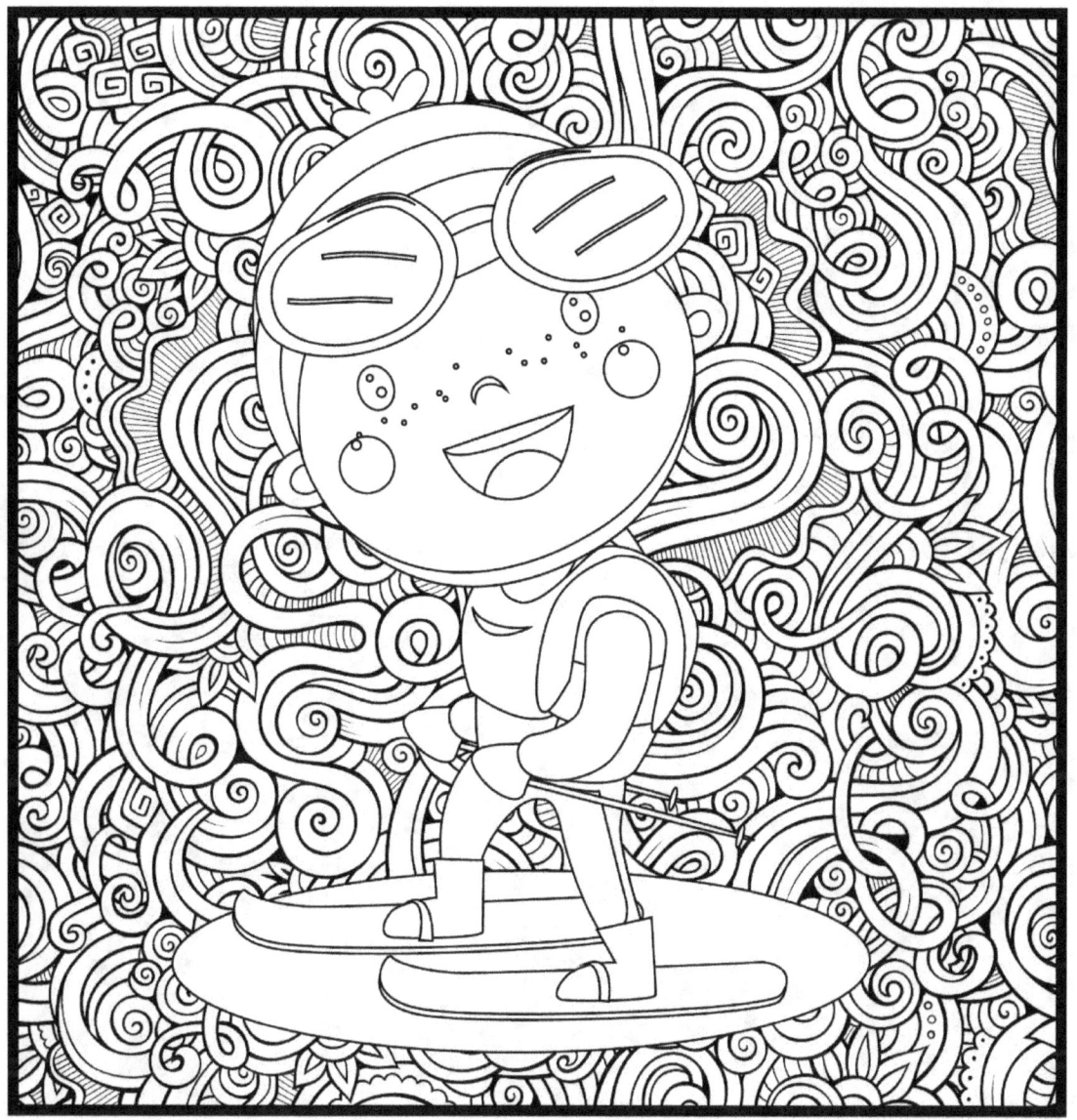

note:

_____

_____

_____

DECEMBER 41TH

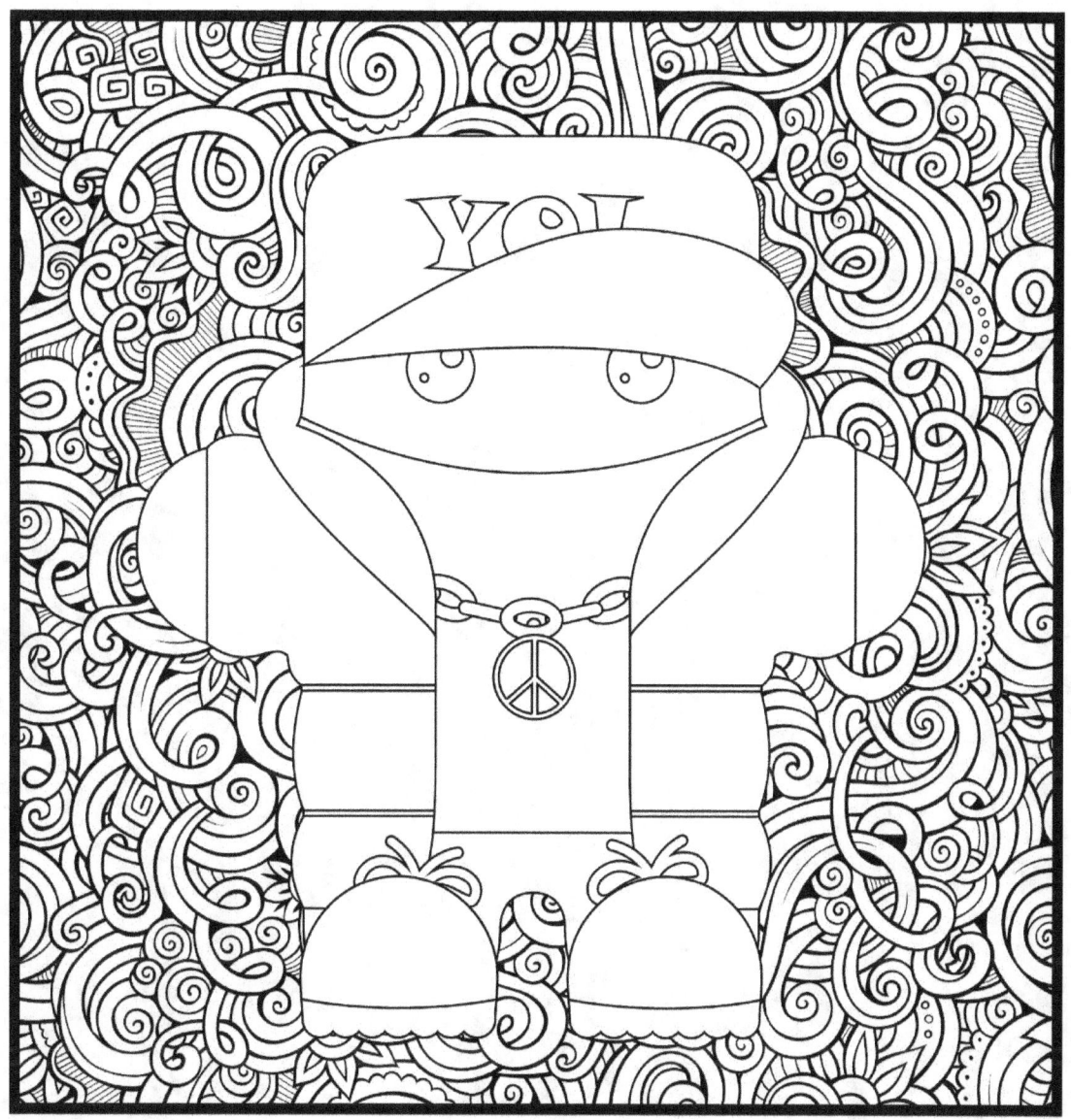

note:

_____

_____

_____

DECEMBER 42TH

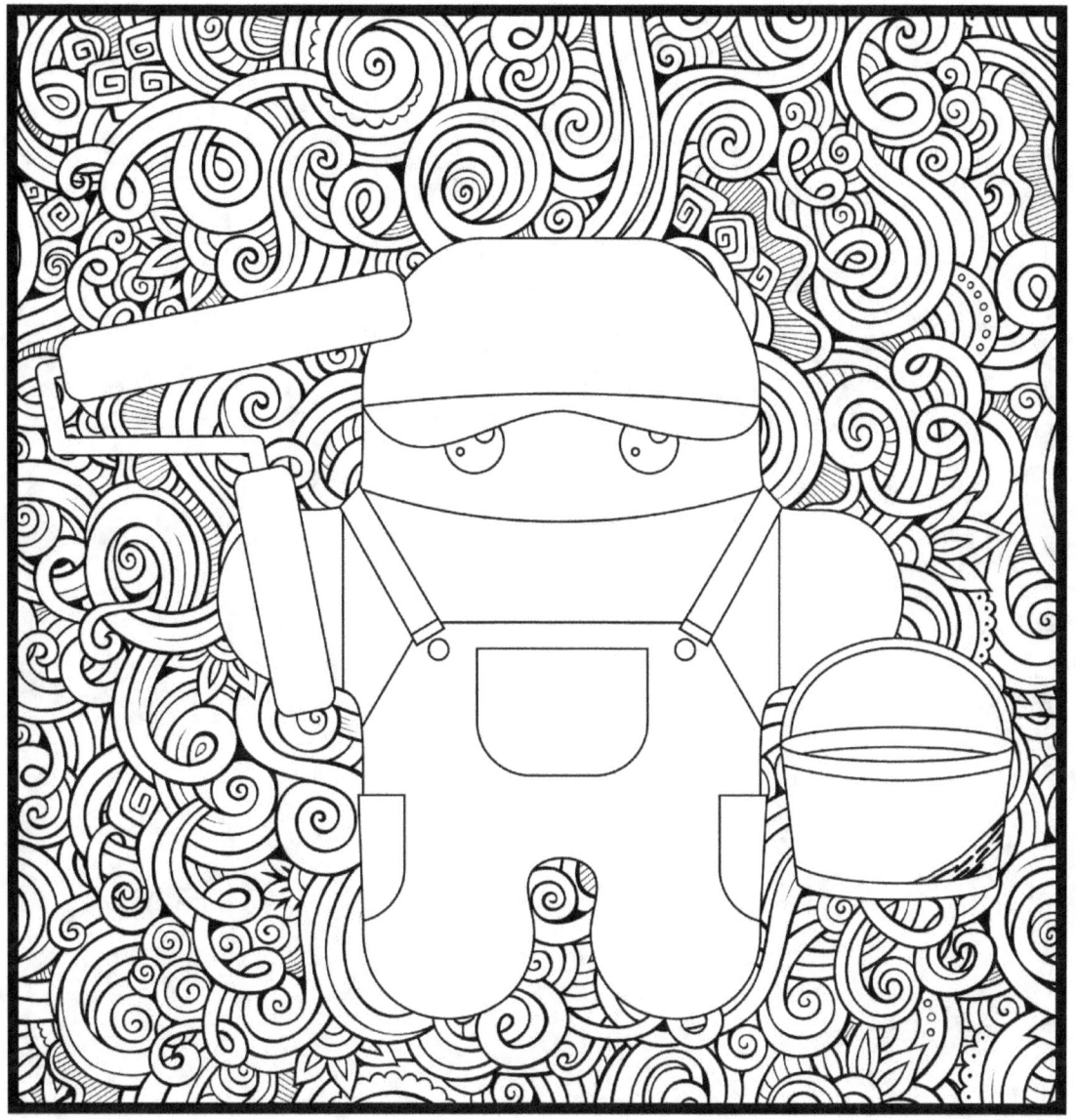

note:

_____

_____

_____

DECEMBER 43TH

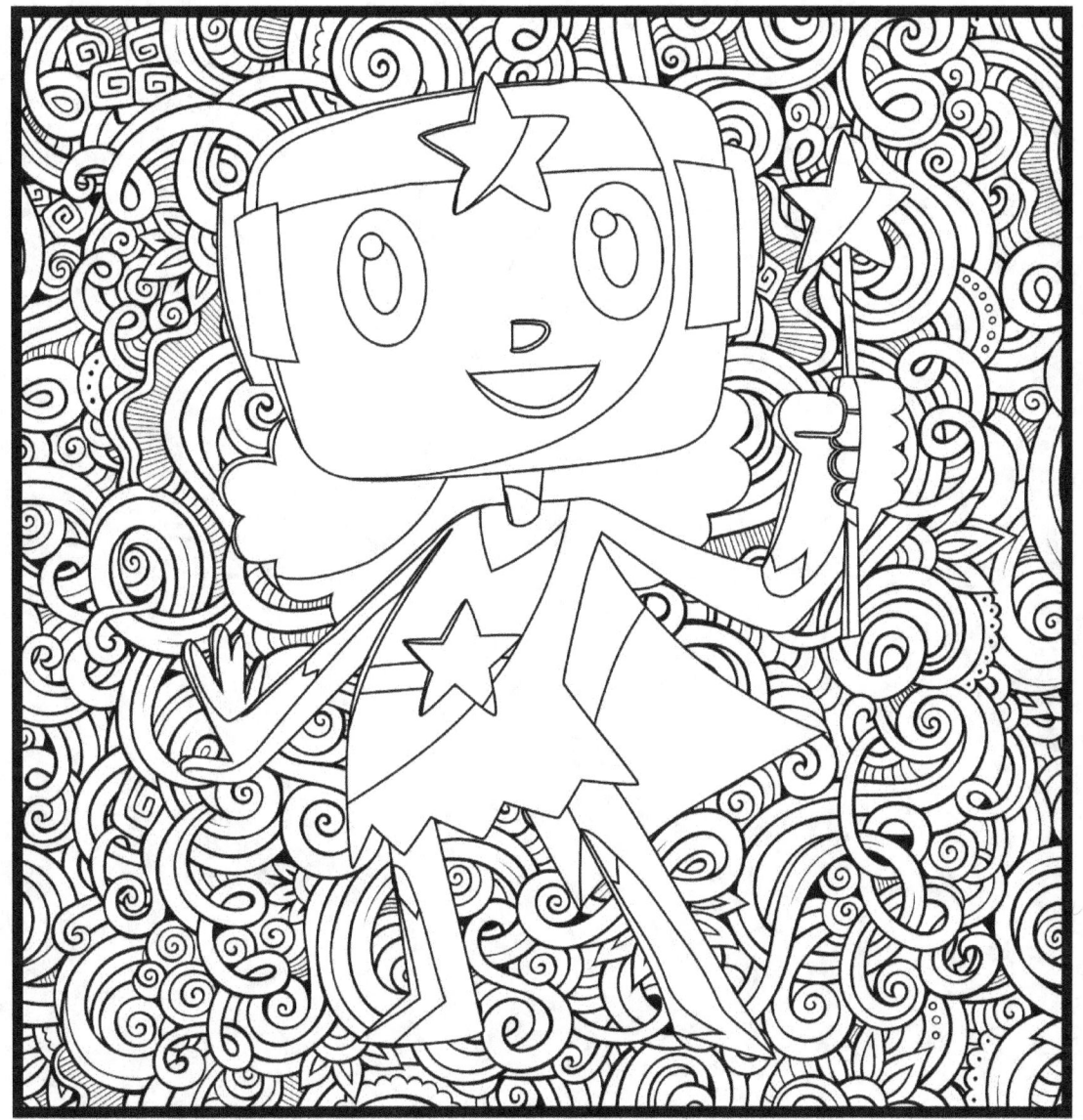

note:

_____

_____

_____

DECEMBER 44TH

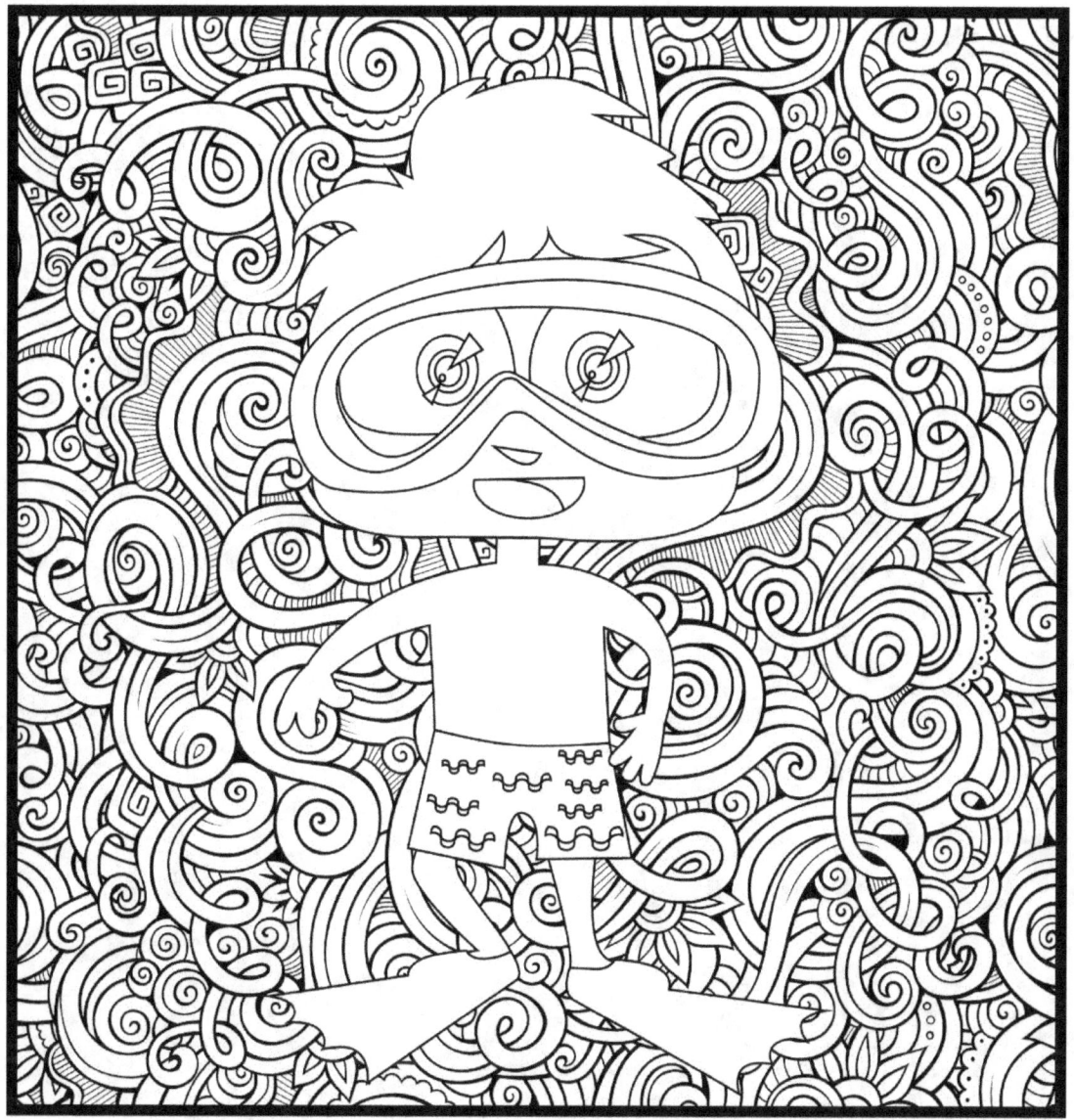

note:
_____
_____
_____

DECEMBER 45TH

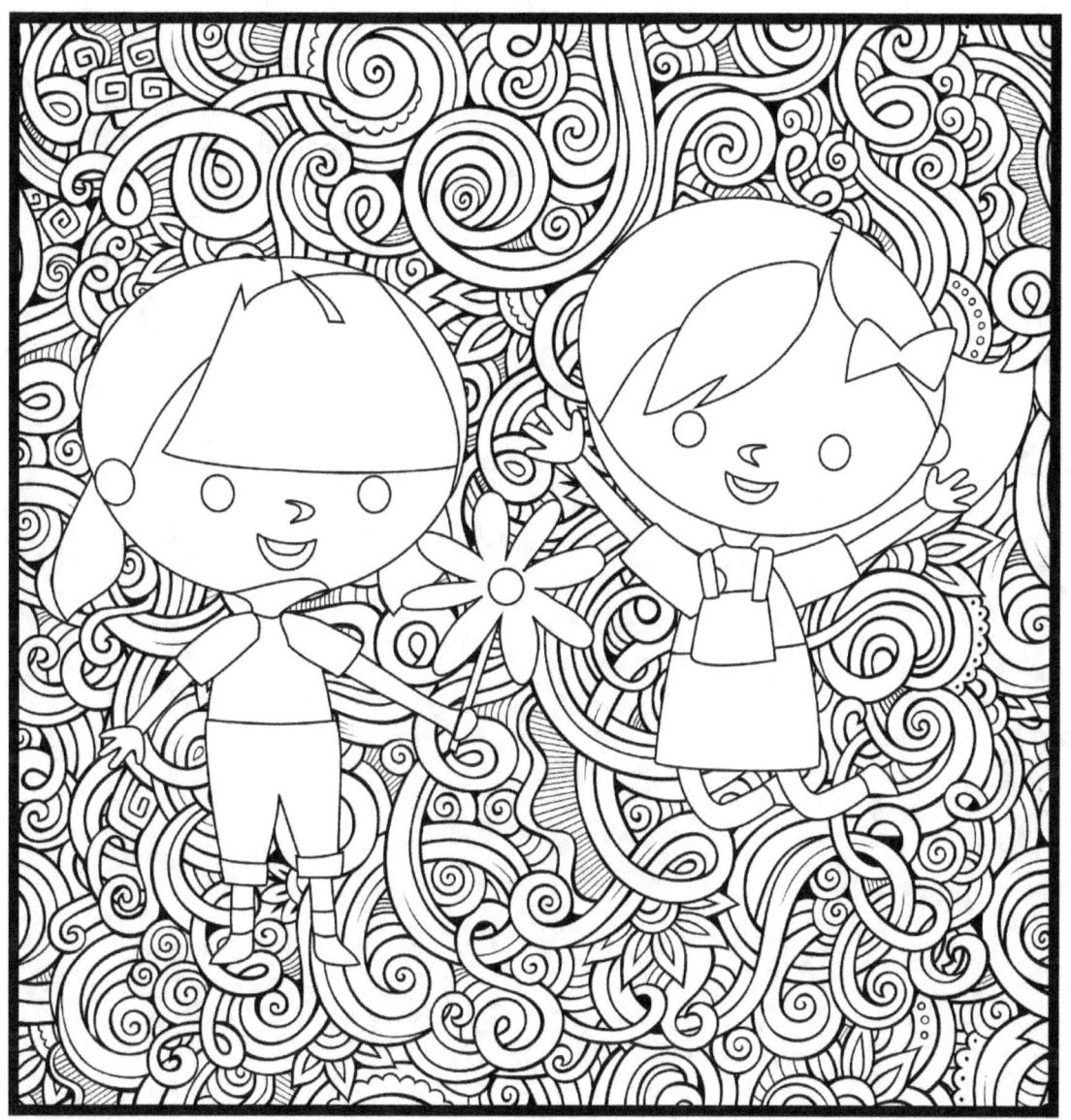

note:

_____

_____

_____

DECEMBER 46TH

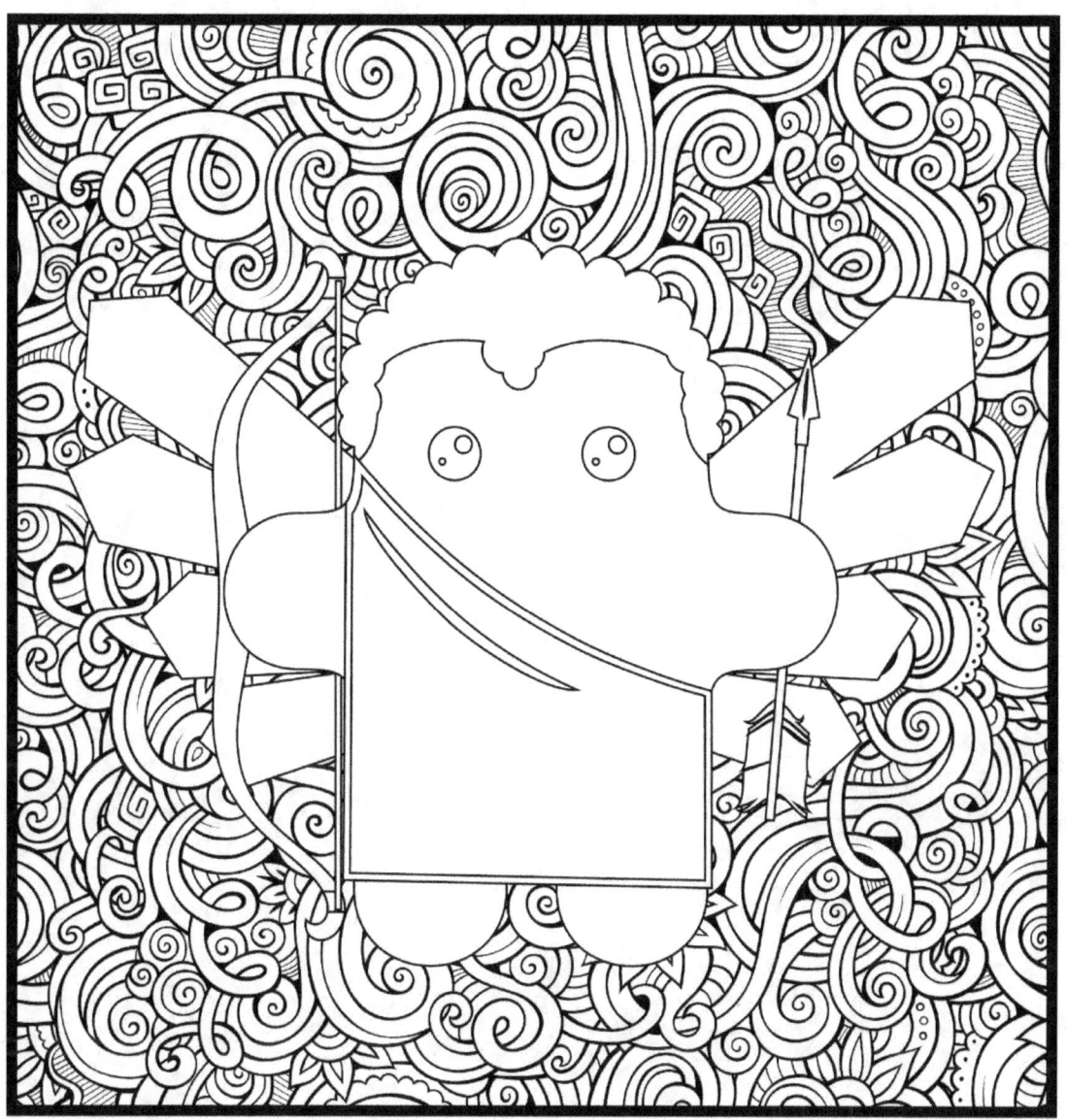

note:

_____

_____

_____

DECEMBER 47TH

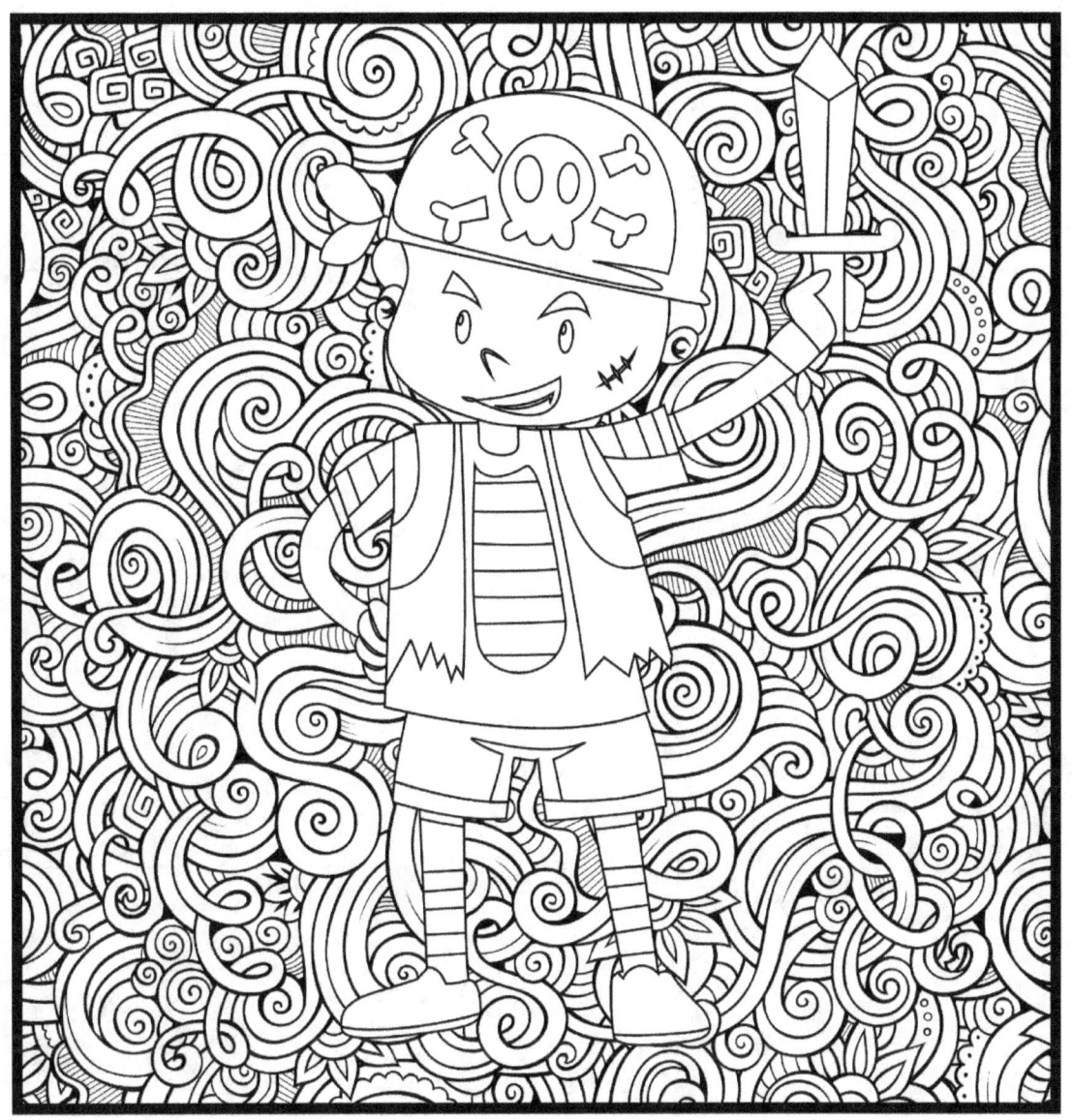

note:

_____

_____

_____

DECEMBER 48TH

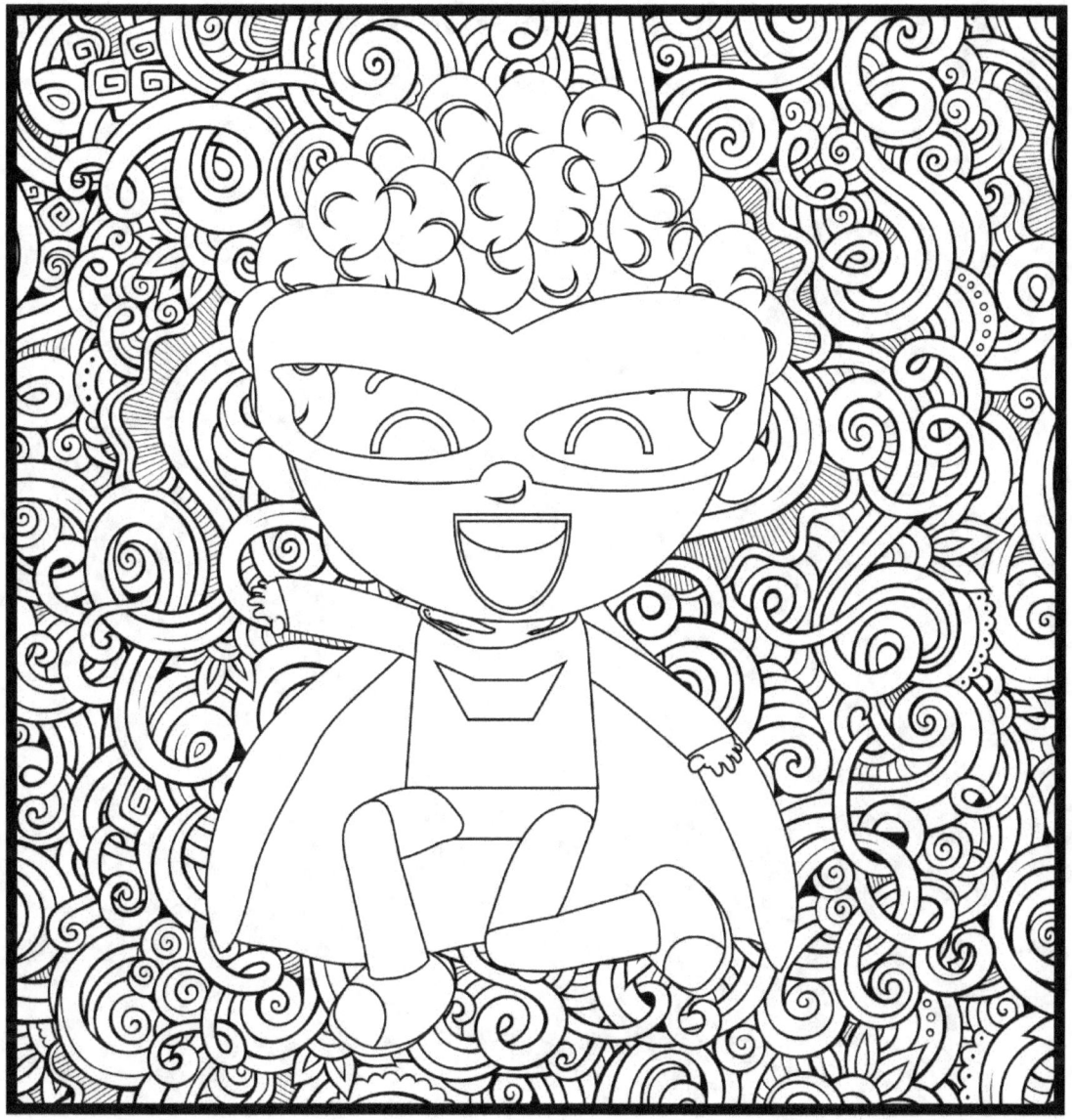

note:

_____

_____

_____

DECEMBER 49TH

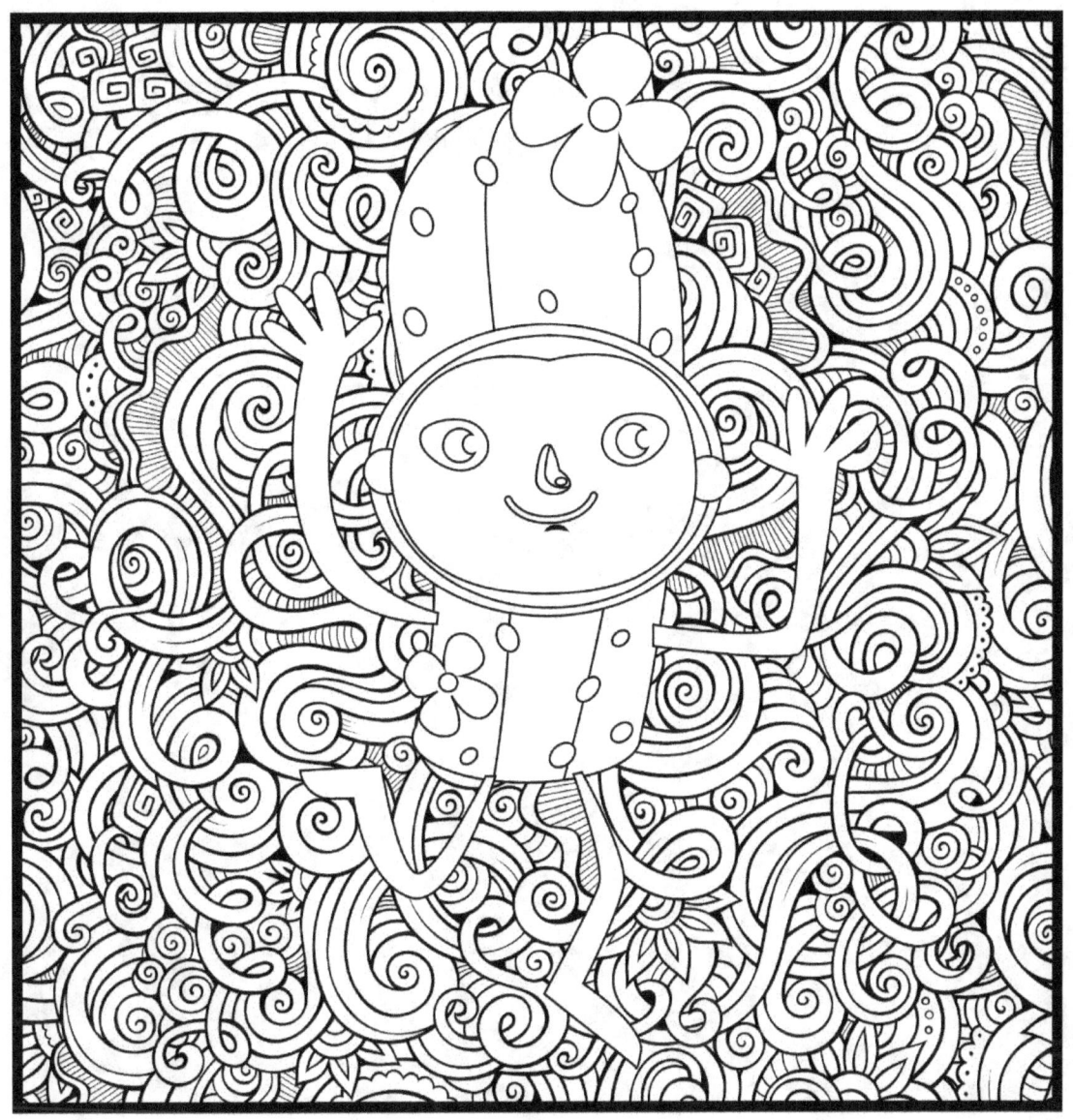

note:

_____

_____

_____

DECEMBER 50TH

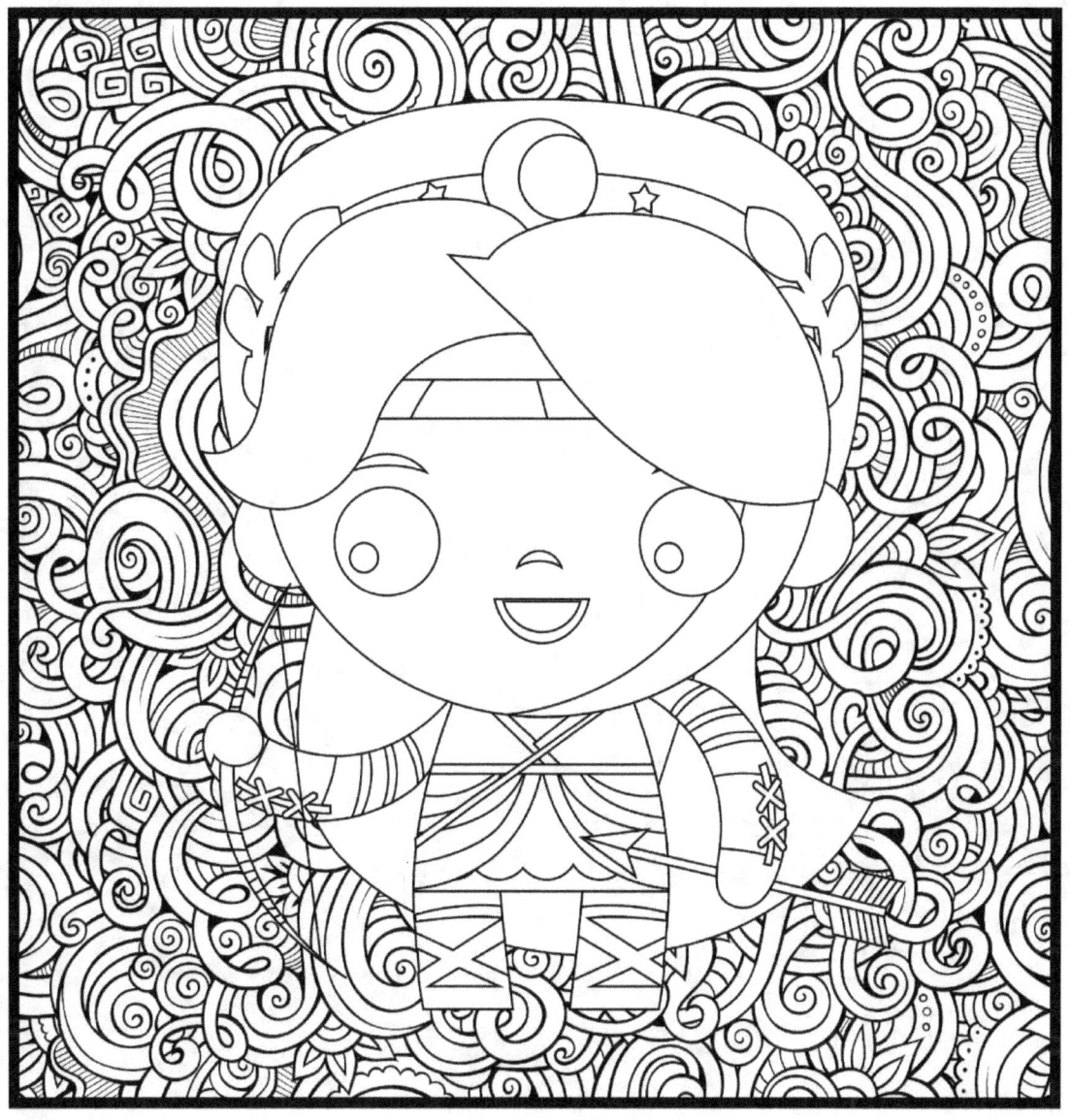

note:

_____

_____

_____